The Steps of Nemesis

Nikolai Evreinov

The Steps of Nemesis
("I know of no such other country …")

A Dramatic Chronicle in Six Scenes from Party Life
in the USSR (1936–1938)

Translated by Zachary Murphy King
Edited by Gleb J. Albert and Sylvia Sasse

DIAPHANES

THINK ART Series of the Institute for Critical Theory (ith)—
Zurich University of the Arts and the Centre for Arts and
Cultural Theory (ZKK)—University of Zurich.

Funded by the Swiss National Science Foundation (SNSF)
and the University of Zurich.

ISBN 978-3-0358-0516-1

Layout: 2edit, Zurich
Printed in Germany

www.diaphanes.com

Contents

Anna Kashina-Evreinova

In Place of a Preface

Non est ad astra mollis
E terris via ...[1]

The play *The Steps of Nemesis* was written by N. N. Evreinov shortly before the outbreak of the war in 1939.[2] I can say with certainty that it was the fruit of the very tense political atmosphere that reigned in Europe, and especially in Russia, in the years preceding the war.

My husband always followed what was happening in his homeland very closely. He read several newspapers of different stripes (including Soviet newspapers) every day, and after the famous trials of the heads of the Communist Party began, that is, from 1936 onward,[3] his habit of reading newspapers and magazines became an almost deranged obsession. And so—at least this is how it seems to me—in order to distance himself from his obsessive ideas about the horrors of Soviet reality, ideas which he himself felt to be unstable, my husband conceived his "dramatic chronicle in six scenes from the party life in the USSR (1936–1938)". He wrote it "for the drawer," understanding that, for the time being, there was no chance that it might be staged.[4] I was the only one to whom he read this play.

He studied everything that could serve as material for the play, approaching this work with his characteristic and rare conscientiousness and persistence. His sources included the thick volume published in Moscow under the title of *Judicial*

Report on the Case of the anti-Soviet "Right Trotskyite" Bloc, more than 700 pages long.* He consulted this book constantly while writing the play over a period of many months.[5] From time to time he visited the journalist Pavel Berlin in order to better verify the documentary material available to him.[6]

In these three years prior to the war, many of our closest friends, believing the promises of Soviet authorities, left for the Soviet Union. I remember in particular our friend and colleague of my husband's, the painter I.I. Bilibin, with whom my husband staged Rimsky-Korsakov's opera *The Tale of Tsar Saltan* twice.[7] The first staging was in Paris, at the Théâtre des Champs-Élysées, and the second a few years later in Prague at the National Theatre. The conductor Mikhail Shteinman, whom my husband "extricated" to Prague in order to direct the opera (the two of them having become close friends not long before that while working on a production of *Ruslan and Lyudmila*, also at the Théâtre des Champs-Élysées), was one of those unable to resist the temptation of the Soviet sirens, and packed his bags to return to the USSR.[8] The composer Sergei Prokofiev,[9] convinced by his wife who loved the "swanky life" of Soviet celebrities, also began to pack his suitcases.**[10]

---

*   *Report of Court Proceedings in the Case of the Anti-Soviet Bloc of Rights and Trotskyites* (Moscow: People's Commissariat of Justice of the U.S.S.R., 1938). [Author's footnote.]

**   I was well aware of their concerns during those months, as we very often met with the Prokofievs and the Shteinmans at that time. My husband was developing a plan with them for the staging of Prokofiev's opera *The Love for Three Oranges*, as Shteinman was negotiating with the Teatro Liceo in Barcelona for its performance in the 1937–38 season. Alas, this production was never brought to fruition. I also want to take the opportunity to express my sympathy for Lina Prokofieva, whose hardships I learned about through the reporting of Edmund Stevens in the American newspaper *The Christian Science Monitor*, "Russia Uncensored," 1949. [Author's footnote.]

It seems that I was the only one who never planned on going "home": in those years I was preparing to become a Christian Science practitioner, an activity which was absolutely unthinkable in the USSR.[11]

My husband seemed to hesitate, agonizingly, over the decision: he deeply loved Russia and his theatrical activities in it.

But a chance encounter resolved all his hesitations.

In the summer of 1937, the Moscow Art Theater arrived at the Paris World's Fair on tour. Naturally, everyone in the Parisian art scene flocked to see them. They performed Trenyov's *Lyubov Yarovaya*, a dramatization of *Anna Karenina* and Gorky's *Enemies*—all of them new productions, never seen abroad. My husband and I decided to buy tickets for the first performance. But at the box office someone from the Russian tour management recognized my husband and we were immediately assigned front row seats for all of the performances, and at the very first intermission we met our old acquaintance, the Soviet writer Victor Fink, whom we had often seen in Petrograd in 1921–1924.[12] He was delighted to see us, immediately asked to visit us, and a day or two later came to our house for dinner. It turned out that he was the head of the Soviet pavilion at the World's Fair in Paris (Fink, if I am not mistaken, served as a soldier in France during the 1914 war and knew French very well).[13] He spent two evenings with us, talking about the life of writers and artists in Russia, and tried to persuade us in every possible way to return "home" ... But, as a result of those conversations, my husband made up his mind: to stay in Paris.

Nemesis, even though she was blindfolded, nevertheless, made many steps during these years, and their sound echoed throughout the world. Some people listen to them with horror, others with hope for a better future ...

After the war, my husband was still unable to see this play performed on stage, or even see it in print. Now this joy falls to me, after accompanying him everywhere over a whole third of a century, in Russia, America, and Europe ...

Paris, July 1955

Nikolai Evreinov

The Steps of Nemesis
("I know of no such other country ...")[14]

**A Dramatic Chronicle in Six Scenes
from Party Life in the USSR (1936–1938)**

CAST

ZINOVIEV, Grigory Yevseevich,[15] former chairman of the Comintern[16] and former chairman of the Northern Commune.[17]

KAMENEV, Lev Borisovich,[18] former chairman of the Council of People's Commissars[19] and the Council of Labor and Defense.[20]

RYKOV, Alexei Ivanovich,[21] former chairman of the Council of People's Commissars.

BUKHARIN, Nikolai Ivanovich,[22] chief editor of the *Izvestiia [News] of the Central Executive Committee of the Union of Soviet Socialist Republics and the All-Union Central Executive Committee of the Soviets*,[23] former chairman of the Comintern, theoretician of Marxism and Leninism.

ZINAIDA Avdeevna Popova,[24] dancer and distant relation of Bukharin.

VARVARA Avdeevna Descourcel,[25] lawyer and distant relation of Bukharin.

STALIN, Iosif Vissarionovich, General Secretary of the All-Union Communist Party of the Bolsheviks.[26]

YAGODA, Genrikh Grigorievich,[27] vice chairman of the OGPU,[28] later people's commissar for domestic affairs.[29]

BULANOV, Pavel Petrovich, personal secretary to G. G. Yagoda and secretary to the People's Commissariat for Domestic Affairs.[30]

YEZHOV, Nikolai Ivanovich,[31] chairman of the Commission for Party Control,[32] later People's Commissar for Domestic Affairs.

RADEK, Karl,[33] former secretary of the Zimmerwald Conference,[34] journalist and consultant to Stalin in foreign affairs.

VYSHINSKY, Andrey Yakovlevich,[35] state prosecutor of the Union of Soviet Socialist Republics.

DOCTOR LEVIN, Lev Grigorievich,[36] senior Kremlin physician and personal physician to Soviet "dignitaries".

LABORATORY ASSISTANT, employee at the GPU's chemical laboratory.[37]

ZAKHAROVNA, NANNY and maid of Zinaida Popova.

GUARDS OF THE NKVD, GUESTS in the home of Z. A. Popova and others.

The events take place in 1936–1938, in Moscow and in its suburb of "Gorki".

First Scene

At the apartment of Zinaida Popova. A large drawing room richly and tastefully furnished, not so much with luxury items as with works of art. Sculptures and exotic flowering plants stand in the corners, and the walls are hung with antique and modern art. Among the latter one work stands out which hangs above the piano: A portrait of the lady of the house depicted as a half-naked dancing nymph.

There are two doors: One opens to the left and leads into the corridor and the foyer, the other opens into the middle of the room through a very wide doorway which leads to a Russian-style dining room with shelves of painted maiolica dishes and antique porcelain, with embroidered cloths[38]on picturesque hooks, a silver samovar and so on. The sliding table which occupies the middle of the dining room is covered with an embroidered table cloth and is surrounded by comfortable seats that resemble armchairs.

Electric lamps illuminate the room with a soft, yet generous light, producing a cozy atmosphere throughout the apartment.

As the curtain goes up we see Zinaida Popova and her sister Varvara Descourcel on the stage, the latter recently arrived from Paris. Both sisters are remarkably, enviably attractive. The older sister, Zinaida, is a beauty with dark red hair, just under thirty years old, and moves with the expressive grace of a professional dancer. Varvara is about 25 years old: a gorgeous blond with a tomboy expression and the air of a "suffragette" in all her body language. Zinaida is dressed in a "homey" tunic-like dress, inventively and garishly colored. Varvara wears a modest, "sporty" Parisian outfit.

ZINAIDA (*relishing her own motherly love for her child, tenderly doting on her one-year-old son in a comfy baby carriage*): Ah goo-goo! Ah-goosiekins! Why aren't you sleeping, sweetie? Hmm? All good children always sleep after midnight and they dream of magical ponies with golden manes, pink hoops that jingle, silver ice skates, funny little puppets and tiny little monkeys dancing on a string. But you're still awake, so you can't see them! Sleep now, my little one, go to sleep! Rock-a-bye! Do you hear that, my little munchkin? Rock-a-bye! It's already almost two.

VARVARA: You call him "little one," "sweetie," "munchkin," but I still don't know what he's really called, even though I'm his aunt. And it's already been two whole weeks since I arrived from France.

ZINAIDA: Just wait, soon we'll have his "Octobering" [39] and give him a name "seriously and for a long time". [40]

VARVARA: What is that supposed to mean, "Octobering"? Is this some kind of red baptism?

ZINAIDA: Yes, but more solemn and ... ideological.

VARVARA: And who have you chosen as the godfather?

ZINAIDA: Genrikh Grigorievich.

VARVARA: Yagoda?

ZINAIDA: Precisely.

VARVARA (*shuddering*): Ughgh!

ZINAIDA: What?

VARVARA: The Chekist-in-chief? [41]

ZINAIDA: Don't be ridiculous! You have a funny way of judging people. First of all, it's a great honor to have such an eminent statesman as a godfather, and second (*laughing*), when it comes to gifts, you can be "dead sure," as Genrikh says, that he'll bring one.

VARVARA: "Dead sure"?! That's a phrase for a Chekist if I ever heard one!

ZINAIDA (*pushing the baby carriage around the room*): You look at everything as an émigré. But for me the main thing is to have a godfather who will keep my son safe. In our life you have to have some insurance, otherwise you're lost.

VARVARA: And if you have to sell your conscience for it?

ZINAIDA: What nonsense! And even if it were true, so what! I'm prepared to do anything for my child! He's my whole life! Don't you understand? If you only knew what sacrifices I've made for him! But it's not worth wasting my breath explaining. My life belongs to him. It's such a joy to have a child, Varya, who clings to you, who's a part of your body, who sticks his arms out and cries "mama," that ...

VARVARA (*interrupting her torrent of words*): Well then, I can only envy you.

ZINAIDA: I can hardly comprehend how I managed without him ... I was always trying to outwit mother nature! I thought that my dancing and art, my whole career as an *artiste*, was the most important thing in the world ... and then it turned out it was all meaningless compared to this little angel (*showers the baby with kisses*), it's impossible to put into words! You should have a child as soon as possible, and learn about the joys of motherhood. And the baby will make your bond with your husband even stronger.

VARVARA (*laughing*): And what about my studies and my law practice? (*Lights a cigarette*).

ZINAIDA: It's nonsense! After all, I sacrificed my choreography.

VARVARA: First of all, you didn't "sacrifice" it at all, since you still perform in the ballet.

ZINAIDA: But that is hardly what I dreamed of!

VARVARA: And secondly, I certainly didn't go to Paris, study at the Sorbonne, and make all the necessary connections, just to throw it all away for ... for a child who might disappoint me when it grows up!

ZINAIDA (*stops with the stroller in the middle of the room*): Oh God, your logic is absurd ... How could my child disappoint me when he's my ... and my husband's, our own flesh and blood! Don't you see, most of all he's a living memory of my departed Sergei Mikhailovich.[42] (*To the baby, snapping her fingers*) A-goo-goo! Goo-goo-goosiekins! Why don't you go to sleep?

VARVARA: That's not what I would say: Your son barely looks like Sergei Mikhailovich ...

ZINAIDA: It's still early to tell now. (*Yelling*) Nanny! Nanny![43]

VARVARA: He was born after your husband's death?

ZINAIDA (*pushing the stroller, putting the baby to sleep*): Yes. Oh it was such an ordeal for me, too much for words! And I would never have gotten over it if my little one hadn't been born, and warmed my lifeless heart with his little body.

VARVARA: Oh God, you really love to give speeches, don't you? I suppose yours is a "theatrical" profession.

ZINAIDA: I'm not "giving a speech" at all! (*Enter the nanny Zakharovna, a woman getting on in her years, with piercing eyes and a strong-willed countenance*).

VARVARA: (*to her sister*): I'm sorry, no offense, but ...

ZINAIDA: (*to the nanny*): He's falling asleep ... You can take him away. Now just bring us the port and two glasses.

NANNY: Yes ma'am! (*Leaves, taking away the stroller with the child*).

VARVARA: Tell me ... poor Sergei Mikhailovich ... was there really no way to save your husband?

ZINAIDA: Oh, I did everything I could! By orders from the very top, he was even treated by doctor Levin, the Kremlin doctor who looks after Stalin himself. But my husband was too shaken by his arrest, all because a friend of his betrayed him, and … his heart couldn't take it. You know, Varya, if it hadn't been for comrade Yagoda, who did everything to ease my husband's stay in the prison hospital!

VARVARA: Yes, yes, you were telling me!

ZINAIDA: … if not for the compassion which he showed to me, how he put himself in my position, I … I would have simply lost my mind!

VARVARA: (*with subtle irony*): And it's since then that he's started paying so much attention to you?

ZINAIDA: What do you mean, "attention"? (*She draws a manicure case towards her and begins doing her nails*).

VARVARA: (*with a hint of mischief in her voice*): Took a shine to you!

ZINAIDA: … My art just made an impression on him, he had already seen me on stage. And after all the fuss about my husband, naturally, I …

VARVARA: (*finishing her sentence*): … hit it off with him.

ZINAIDA: He really loves performers, actors and …

VARVARA: … especially actresses, I've heard. And since he's omnipotent, everyone falls at his feet? And you too?

ZINAIDA: Not at all! He doesn't stand on ceremony when you talk to him. But it's true, I was a little afraid of him at first: of course you know Yagoda is the most powerful man in the USSR after Stalin. Head of the GPU, that's nothing to be sneezed at! But when I got to know him, it turned out he's not only a down-to-earth soul, but also a comrade who's ready to make any sacrifice for the ones he loves.

VARVARA: (*sarcastically*): And what does his wife think about his "sacrifices"?

(*The telephone rings. Pause*).

VARVARA (*runs to the telephone and picks up the receiver*): Nikolai Ivanych?[44] Hello, uncle! (*To her sister*) It's Bukharin calling from the newspaper. (*Into the receiver*) No, we haven't gone to bed yet! We're waiting for you ... tired and hungry? ... Well of course! ... You went straight from the trial to the editorial office?[45]... I can imagine! (*After a pause*) OK! (*To her sister*) He's coming with Rykov; uncle's waiting for him to arrive; he wants us to make him something to eat. (*Listens*) Ah, Radek's joining us as well? ... And Genrikh Grigorievich? ... Wonderful! ... We'll be expecting you! (*Hangs up the receiver*).

ZINAIDA (*jumping up*): Why didn't you ask how the trial ended?

VARVARA: Ah, I completely forgot!

ZINAIDA (*sitting back down*): Radek demanded the death penalty for them, in the newspaper, but ... That's all just words, I'm sure of it.[46]

VARVARA: Is it true what he told me, that your place is a "conspiratorial apartment"?

ZINAIDA: What's "conspiratorial" supposed to mean?! Karl Radek is always making jokes, and ... exaggerates to get some laughs! That's why there's even a rumor that all the jokes in Moscow come out of his mouth.[47]

VARVARA: He's so funny! At the last party he said to me (*imitating a Polish-German accent*): "We'll have to resort to conspiracy: since your sister is refusing to perform for us, we'll act as if we're leaving. Agreed?" And then I said to him: "And why are you calling it a conspiracy? My sister will dance for us anyways, if I ask her to". "I don't think so," he says, "but if Yagoda asks her, that's different. But since he's not here, we'll have to resort to conspiracy, after all this is a conspiratorial apartment". "Conspiratorial?" I ask. "Oh, you didn't know?" he says, laughing, "I just told you everything didn't I!"

ZINAIDA: He's always laughing, that Radek! He only wants to make jokes.

VARVARA: Why have you still not introduced me to Yagoda after all this time?

ZINAIDA: It's hardly been a week since you got here. And he's a terribly busy man! After all the whole investigation of the "Zinoviev bloc"[48] was prepared by the GPU, and Yagoda is their immediate superior.

VARVARA (*with a hint of contempt*): Well naturally, the "Chekist in chief"!

ZINAIDA: More like the "ever-vigilant eye of the proletariat"! And besides, as Stalin said, "we're all Chekists".

VARVARA: All the worse for Russia!

ZINAIDA: What do you know! You're biased, you see it from an émigré point of view and believe all the gossip.

VARVARA (*angry*): Ah, so it's just "gossip" that he has everyone he wants taken out to be shot?! "Gossip" that he has people working like serfs in concentration camps,[49] where he has prisoners doing forced labor in the lumber and fishing industries?! And that Belomor canal he built on the bones of toiling intellectuals?![50] And Narym and Solovki, and all the horrific things happening there?[51] And you defend a butcher like this Yagoda? And you're even in love with him, I can see it. It's all just revolting!

ZINAIDA (*laughing artificially*): Well there you go! You shouldn't be a lawyer, you should be a prosecutor! Really, you would convict everyone. You only forgot one thing: All the yarns spun up by your Parisian hacks, that's one thing, but what Maxim Gorky says about Genrikh Yagoda will have a completely different place in the pages of history![52] (*Taking a lavishly produced illustrated volume from the nearest shelf*).[53] Look, just read the foreword to this monograph on that very same Belomor canal, for which Yagoda was awarded the Order of Lenin. (*Reads*) "You have accomplished something great, something massive," writes

Gorky, "this book explains how enemies of the proletariat were reeducated into fellow laborers and comrades-in-arms".[54]

VARVARA: For me, Gorky is not God: He can be mistaken!

ZINAIDA: And what about the "voice of the people"? Did you read what 7,000 communards from the "Yagoda Labor Commune of the GPU in Bolshevo" said?[55]

VARVARA (*smiling*): And where would I have read that?! Anyways, your newspapers are so boring that ...

ZINAIDA (*recites with pathos*):

"And if the savage might of foes
Should surround us like a ring,
We'll rise, a valiant army on the wing,
For leading us to fight will be Yagoda!"[56]

VARVARA: Oh God, how you all love to recite and give speeches here! You huff and puff and speechify and eulogize ... And you walk around in rags after twenty years of "revolutionary conquest," and you need to work half a year to afford a pair of boots. You say I don't know what I'm talking about, but there's no "shoe" to fit this place! (*The nanny Zakharovna enters, with a bottle of port and two glasses*).

ZINAIDA (*to her sister, with forced laughter*): No no, don't you wriggle out of the fight! (*To the nanny, pointing to a small table*): Put it here! (*She obeys*). Just ask the nanny (*pours liquid into the glasses*), she only just came back from the camps,[57] I'm vouching for her, under the protection of that very same Yagoda ... Tell her, Zakharovna,[58] what do they say in the concentration camp about Genrikh Grigorievich? Do they criticize him, praise him? Be completely honest. (*To her sister*): Drink!

VARVARA: I don't want to. (*Extends the glass to the nanny*): Would you like some? (*Passes her the glass*).

NANNY (*bowing*): Thank you, Varvara Avdeevna! (*To the older sister*) Genrikh Grigorievich is a real somebody and the master of the Russian land![59] And who am I to tell about him? (*Drinks from the glass and sets it down in its former place*).

ZINAIDA: Well there you go! Everyone can think for themselves.

NANNY (*wiping her mouth with her hand, squinting her eyes*): You couldn't say anything but good things about him. And I'll spend the rest of my days in praise to the Lord for what he done takin' me out of that vale of tears. (*Wipes her eyes and blows her nose*). I will say though: they send a body away to these "concentration" camps, and for what? For the Christian faith! What kind of reason is that? They'll feel God's wrath for that! Mark my words!

ZINAIDA (*laughing and mocking her*): Who? The Godless ones?[60] Stalin? The GPU? (*The telephone rings*).

VARVARA (*runs to the telephone, answers it*): Hello! Whom do you want to speak to? Is comrade Bukharin here? No, not yet, why? Yes, yes, this is Popova's apartment! Bukharin must still be at the newspaper office. With whom do I have the pleasure? Marshal Tukhachevsky's office?[61] And, I'm sorry, what is the matter? No, he's not expected today. It's already dark out ... What? How's that? (*Hangs up*). Hung up!

ZINAIDA (*to her sister*): You really shouldn't be so forthcoming on the phone ... We may have protection, but ... there are plenty of provocateurs in Moscow, after all!

VARVARA (*jokingly*): Duly noted! (*To the nanny*): So, you say God will punish the atheists?

NANNY: Certainly! But, of course, not their hired servants, but only those who give them orders ... It was not so long ago, when Lenin was struck with paralysis, one godless orator mocked God. "Look," he says, "Comrades, watch me blaspheme God himself! And nothing will happen to me: I'm still in my right mind, and my tongue doesn't falter, and my arms and legs all work just fine. If God exists, why doesn't He punish me?! Well, because there is no such thing as God and I remain unscathed ... (*The doorbell rings in the entryway*).

ZINAIDA: (*starting to stand up*): They're here!

NANNY: I'll go let them in!

ZINAIDA: Wait a minute, I want to go look in the peephole first! It's an evil hour. (*Runs out to the left*).

VARVARA: (*to the nanny*): So what happened? Did the atheist have his fun without any consequences?

NANNY: That orator was just a hired servant. But the man who sent him to blaspheme against God—that Lenin—he had his wits and his words taken by God, and he struck him paralyzed. The long and short of it is: He smote him down.

ZINAIDA (*returning*): It's Radek ... Let him in, nanny!

NANNY (*exiting left*): Right away! (*Exits*).

ZINAIDA (*heading to the dining room*): Keep him entertained, Varya! I'll prepare everything for dinner. (*Closes the sliding doors*).

VARVARA And what is his *position sociale*, can you remind me?

ZINAIDA (*stopping at the threshold*): Radek's? He was famous as Lenin's emissary in the days of the German Revolution ...[62] former secretary of the Zimmerwald Conference ... official journalist and spokesman for the Communist Party and, finally—don't you know?—Stalin's advisor for foreign affairs.

VARVARA (*with a smirk*): So, a real bigwig. Why didn't you just say so!

ZINAIDA (*smiling*): That's exactly what I'm saying! (*Exits into the dining room, closing the sliding doors behind her at precisely the moment when Radek appears from the left, accompanied by Zakharovna. He is short, almost dwarf-like, and resembles a good-natured chimpanzee; he is dressed in an outfit that at least attempts to meet an idea of European chic: a velvet sport coat and stylish slacks. He has an ingratiating demeanor, "clever" eyes, a jaundiced tinge to his face and a sarcastic smile that never leaves his lips. His speech immediately betrays the accent of a Galician polyglot and, specifically, a Pole).*

RADEK (*greeting Varya*): Good evening, Comrade! (*They shake hands*). No sign of Bukharin yet? So I'm the first … How do you do? Are you settling in to our Moscow? Do you like it, after Paris?

VARVARA (*smiling acidly*): Not especially.

RADEK: Haven't found the Bolsheviks to your liking? Is that it? We're such a rowdy bunch … Don't allow Europe to get a wink of sleep … *Vous avez raison!* And we're so serious! We lack that French "tralala" and "après moi le déluge"!

NANNY (*tipsy, waves her hand at him*): You're a godless one, that's right! Worse than any "tralala"! Made yourself an idol out of Lenin and you kiss the murderer as if he were Christ's icon!

RADEK: "Icon"?! Oh, qu'elle est amusante! (*The nanny waves her hand and exits into the dining room, closing the door behind her*).

VARVARA: Please take a seat!

RADEK: Merci! (*They sit down across from each other*).

VARVARA: Tell me, what sentence did they give to those Oppositionists?

RADEK: To be shot, chère madame! To be shot! That was Stalin's wish.

VARVARA: My sister claims you were the first to demand in the papers that they be shot.

RADEK: What do you mean "I demanded"?! Think, what if I hadn't demanded it? Do you think it would have turned out differently? You know, it's only chickens that think the sun rises thanks to the cock's crow! But the sun manages without any cock-a-doodle-doo and maybe is even better without it.

VARVARA: Then why did you call for this in the papers?

RADEK: That they be shot?! (*Chuckles*): And why do we all now inform on each other and treacherously betray people with "a cynicism that comes to equal grace," as Saltykov said?[63] The reason, is that if one person doesn't snitch, another will do it for him ... So it's better that I call for them to be shot before someone else thinks of it.

VARVARA (*laughing*): What strange logic!

RADEK (*mockingly*): Not at all! It is actually perfectly natural logic, given the primitive form of thought typical of "the age of Stalin".

VARVARA: Which is ...? What do you mean?

RADEK: Take the Eskimos for example. Long ago, they had a rich, developed language, when they still lived in a temperate climate. But when they were driven towards the Arctic ocean, i.e. into *primitive* conditions where they had to simply survive, their life became so simple that the necessity for their rich language, with its complex concepts, gradually fell away. Something similar happened to us under Stalin, who drove the Communist Party to such primitive concepts that he forced it to forget the language of Karl Marx and all his philosophy.

VARVARA (*giggling*): And what a brave man you are to honor your dictator like this! Aren't you afraid I'll tell on you?

RADEK (*laughing*): To whom? The GPU? The head of the GPU is with us, he's with the Oppositionists.

VARVARA: Comrade Yagoda? Are you serious?

ZINAIDA (*emerging from the dining room, a little dressed up and leaving the doors open: in the other room the nanny is busily setting the table, laying out hors d'œuvres and so forth*): Hello, dear comrade! How's life? (*They shake hands*).

RADEK (*being witty*): For now I still have one, although every day I risk waking up shot.

ZINAIDA (*to her sister, jokingly*): For God's sake, don't listen to a word he says! He loves to subvert everything, it's terrifying to watch if you don't know him. (*To him*): Well, how did the trial go? You must have come directly from court? What was the sentence?

RADEK (*clears his throat*): Death.

ZINAIDA (*her expression becomes serious*): To be shot?! Are you ... joking?

RADEK: Not at all! Why are you surprised?

ZINAIDA: But how? The architects of Russia's destiny have been sentenced to be shot like riff-raff, and I'm not supposed to be surprised?! These men stood at the helm of Russia's government for twenty years.

RADEK: And so what? The longer they were on top, the more mistakes they made.

ZINAIDA (*deeply upset*): No, this can't be happening! This is absurd!

VARVARA (*to her, angrily*): You could stop bragging about how no other country has rulers like Soviet Russia: how they are incorruptible, and heroes of labor, and how they stand on the night watch of the revolution without fail. And it turns out they're the same "riff-raff" as everywhere else: murderers, spies, saboteurs ready to sell Russia for thirty pieces of silver. And they forced the entire population to kneel down to this kind of authority in "one sixth-part of the globe"? These vile "dogs" sent innocent people into exile, forced the peasants into destitution, executed them and forbid them from praying to God, took away all belongings from people, freedom of thought, speech, movement, and the whole time Europe stood by and applauded this diabolical farce and signed treaties with these bandits!

ZINAIDA (*dejected, with a wave of the hand*): You always take this biased view: you roll everything together and paint it with the same brush! Just the fact that, in the USSR, they finally got these crooks, should be enough to make you stop and think for a minute ... That's what makes Soviet power different, it ...

VARVARA (*interrupting her*): What a great government that you have to shoot everyone in it as thanks for twenty years of service!

ZINAIDA (*biting her lips*): The Tsar and the Tsar's ministers also had to be shot![64]

VARVARA: First, don't say such filth, and second, be reasonable: the Tsar was shot by his enemies, while Zinoviev and Kamenev were shot by their own comrades.

RADEK (*laughing nervously*): Hold on, madam, they haven't shot them yet! Maybe Stalin will forgive them! After all, he's like our Tsar now. And his power is even more unlimited, although he's a very limited man. (*As he says this last line, we hear the sound of doors opening and closing in the hallway, footsteps and indistinct voices. Enter, from the left, Bukharin with a briefcase and Rykov, without. Bukharin represents a type known as the "eternal student": as if he just finished a game of cricket, as the writer Mariengof described him.[65] Bald, with a sharply pointed goatee. Something satirical and merciless flickers in the feverish expression of this fifty-year-old neurasthenic, always knowing and staying within his limits. Not much to look at, he quickly comes alive when he starts to talk about a subject in his purview: it's not for nothing that his erudition, inspiration, gift for oratory and characteris-*

tic wit made him into a figure of authority and gave him an aura of enchantment among his comrades in the party. Rykov is completely different: tall, boney, with a goatee like Anton Chekhov's, wearing a sport coat of an old-fashioned cut and an unfashionable starched collar, his trousers tucked into "Russian boots," this distinguished Bolshevik, at the age of 55, reminds one of a "village schoolteacher" with a weakness for drink and a habit of chuckling whether he has reason to or not. He speaks with a stutter.[66]

BUKHARIN (*as he enters, kisses his nieces and shakes Radek's hand*): Well, naturally! Radek is already winning the ladies' hearts with his famous wordplay! Nothing holds him back! Hello, Karlusha, the "grinning Galician"! (*To Varvara, pointing to Rykov*): Have you met? I can't remember.

VARVARA (*greeting Rykov*): Comrade Rykov? How could I forget! I even recall that vodka was renamed in his honor.

RYKOV (*laughing*): And what do you think? Thanks to "Rykovka" I'm immortal.[67] And I'm quite proud of it. For "drinking is the joy of the Rus',"[68] and in our day you couldn't get by without it! Otherwise, with everything happening all around us, you'd have to hang yourself!

RADEK: Why "hang yourself"? That's out of style! The hot new thing is "getting shot"! (*General laughter*).

ZINAIDA (*pointing towards the dining room*): This way please, my honored guests ...

BUKHARIN (*interrupting her*): No, Zina, we must wait for Yagoda! He said he would be late. (*Lights a papirosa*[69] *and lights Radek's pipe*).

RYKOV (*flicking his collar with a finger*): But I wouldn't mind "taking the edge off" right away, for "the spirit is strong, but the flesh is weak".

ZINAIDA AND VARVARA (*all at once*): Well what's stopping you?! This way! Our stomachs are growling too. (*They take*

Rykov by the arm and lead him into the dining room, where they serve him and have something to eat themselves).

BUKHARIN (*to Radek*): Well, what do you have to say about this idiotic treachery?

RADEK: You mean Zinoviev and Kamenev?

BUKHARIN: Trying to "set us up" as part of the plot, as if it might save them. Fools![70]

RADEK: Don't take it to heart, my little Bukharinkin! It's just a trick to delay their sentence. The court probably understood that. What's really mysterious is why in the hell they all admitted to something of which they were totally innocent.

BUKHARIN: Completely incomprehensible why on earth they slandered themselves before the entire world and not only didn't defend themselves, but almost begged to be shot. I don't think there's been anything like it since the creation of the world!

RADEK: Well, they were made to by Yagoda. I mean, he was the one who oversaw the investigation with the prosecutor Vyshinsky.

BUKHARIN: And why on earth did Yagoda need to do that?!

RADEK: Because he acts according to Stalin's bidding.

BUKHARIN: Maybe he does! But why did Stalin suddenly feel the urge to have his former associates declare themselves to be criminals in the eyes of the entire world?

RADEK: What do you mean why?! Because Stalin isn't in any danger from the Oppositionists, the danger is from the workers and peasants who resent being forced into working like serfs at the factories and collective farms.

BUKHARIN: What are you trying to say?

RADEK: That he had to redirect the resentment of the masses on a false trail: It wasn't Stalin's fault that the five-year-plans failed and there are shortages in everything for the exploited proletariat, it was wreckers like Zinoviev, Kamenev and their ilk ... Don't you understand?

BUKHARIN (*nervously pacing around the room and smoking like a chimney*): Damn it! I would like to see for myself how they could make me pour rotten garbage on my own head in public.

RADEK: Yessir, it's not a pretty picture!

BUKHARIN: ... To admit to vile, debased, disgusting acts! And even more, to do it almost ecstatically! I swear on my honor, I would rather be hanged, quartered and put to death under a dull saw!

RADEK: Not everyone is so brave, my dear Bukharin'ka.

BUKHARIN: Could they really not have preferred suicide to this self-flagellation on a planetary scale?!

RADEK: But you are forgetting what Trotsky said in a candid moment?[71] "Under the conditions of Soviet interrogation, suicide is an inaccessible luxury".[72]

RYKOV (*returning to his comrades, chewing the last bite of a piece of bread as he bows to the hostess with clownish ceremoniousness*): What is this "inaccessible luxury" you are chewing over here?

BUKHARIN: Suicide.

RYKOV (*laughing, with a blissful expression*): What a bunch of bull! Be like me, drink: that's suicide on the installment plan! What's inaccessible about that?! (*Zinaida carries in a tray with a bottle of burgundy, cognac, glasses and canapes with caviar; she sets all this on the small table next to the bottle of port and exits into the dining room*).

RADEK (*to Rykov*): You, my friend, you are talking like that engineer who declared that "the *future* of our technology still lies *before* us". (*Laughs; so does Rykov. Both of them approach the table, pour themselves some cognac and eat a canape*).

Bukharin (*nervously*): That's enough clowning, comrades! We didn't come here to chew the fat. We came here to decide: how are we going to respond to these backstabbing dogs?

Radek: Zinoviev and Kamenev?

Bukharin: Do you think it was easy for me to edit today's *Izvestiia*, with a denunciation against me printed there in black and white, calling me a counter revolutionary?![73]

Rykov: Hyeah … something must be done about it!

Radek (*caustically*): And what exactly should that be, when it all depends on whether they want to liquidate us or not? If "management" decides to get rid of an employee, whatever he tries to do will be completely pointless. There was an employee, I heard, that was always late to work; they warned him he would be fired for malicious *negligence*. So he started arriving more punctually, for which the same management accused him of jarring *officiousness*. And when he started arriving even before the prescribed time, they …

Bukharin (*finishing his sentence*): Fired him for flagrant *careerism*. Isn't that right? I've heard that one already! Got anything fresh?

Radek (*squinting*): How? So someone's paid a visit to Marshal Tukhachevsky?!

Bukharin (*a little confused*): What does this have to do with Tukhachevsky?

Radek: Because it happens that he is the *only one* who's heard me tell that joke. Which means you couldn't have heard it from anyone else but him.

Bukharin: Well, and so what?

Radek: Here's what: Marshal Tukhachevsky and his group are only supposed to contact us through third parties. This was decided at the very beginning of our collective actions against Stalin.

RYKOV: Quite right, because if we rub shoulders with them we could draw attention to ourselves and our co-conspirators.

BUKHARIN (*to Radek*): Well, if you must know, I didn't seek out a meeting with Tukhachevsky. He came to me.

RADEK: Even better? And what did he do that for?

BUKHARIN: To confer with me.

RADEK: Regarding what?

BUKHARIN: Are you "playing dumb"? As if you don't know perfectly well.

RADEK: Ugh, you, *Donnerwetter!*[74] We're surrounded by informants on all sides, and while we're trying to get a grip on Stalin, *he* will lay hold of us ten times! The whole apparatus of power is in his hands!

BUKHARIN: Bullshit! You know why? Because Yagoda is with us, and the GPU is everything!

RADEK: And Stalin has Yezhov, who's got his sights set on Yagoda's spot!

BUKHARIN: So let him try! His arms won't reach! (*During the last few lines the sound of the lock clicking and the door opening can be heard from the left; at the same time as Bukharin recites his last lines, Genrikh Yagoda enters from the hallway. He is a gaunt man with brown hair, medium height, 45 years old, relatively handsome, with a face the pallor of tobacco, a delicate mustache and eyes that always seem to be taking aim at their object. "Nasty tongues" were not far from the truth when they said that he is a "Mephistopheles from the pale of settlement". Yagoda is wearing a military coat, with a revolver on his belt and cavalry trousers tucked into elegant high boots. He is carrying a voluminous briefcase under his arm. It is obvious the head of the GPU is out to impress with his martial chic and icy "affected" politeness. When that "ice" breaks, however, it reveals an absolutely insolent, rude temperament that knows no limit when enraged. He is a hardened cynic of the "predatory" variety, although he tries to pretend his cynicism is only for show, and that behind it lie whatever qualities would be fitting for an Übermensch*).

YAGODA (*greeting everyone*): I see you're talking again about Yezhov and his little paws? This little midget is all anyone ever talks about. As if there were nothing better to talk about than this "turd in the grass"!

RYKOV (*greeting him*): What do you mean?

YAGODA: "A turd in the grass"? That's when you're walking through a meadow and you don't notice where some dog took a shit. One step and BAM! You slip and you're in it! (*All laugh*).

RADEK (*to him*): You came in without ringing?

BUKHARIN: He has a key, just like I do.

RYKOV (*and the others, crowding around Yagoda*): Well, Genrikh, don't keep us waiting: tell it to us straight, why did they all confess in court and sentence themselves to be shot?

BUKHARIN (*to Yagoda*): So is it true you torture them there at the Lubyanka?[75]

RADEK: Wasn't it *you* that ran the investigation together with the prosecutor?

YAGODA (*trying to fight free*): Ach, come on boys! Just wait a minute! Don't squawk at me all at once! Let me catch my breath here! I just spoke to the *big guy himself*.

RYKOV: With "daring Joe"?

BUKHARIN: Did you see him?

YAGODA: On the telephone. Hard to please! Asked me to come see him tomorrow. I have a feeling, he's going to give me hell ... (*Seeing the bottles*): Aah, burgundy! A swig of that will fortify me. (*Radek pours him a glass, which Yagoda drinks down thirstily*).

BUKHARIN: No, really! What do they do in your dungeons to get people to confess to things they haven't even done?

RYKOV: That's obvious: they torture them. How else could you explain it!

YAGODA: Ahh, comrades, what do you mean, "torture"? Just hearing it makes me laugh! If a man smokes, for example, a hundred cigarettes a day, or is (*looks at Rykov*) has a taste for spirits, just leave them for a day without tobacco and "Rykovka" and watch what they're capable of! (*Everyone laughs*). Or, say a man wants to go to sleep, but they interrogate him day and night for 12 hours at a time. Is that really "torture"? (*Everyone laughs*).

BUKHARIN: But what are we supposed to call "torture" then, I'd like to know?

YAGODA: That's a horse of a different color! I don't want to talk out of school about secrets of the profession. The work of a chekist is also an art. And for us, like for any true artists, I'm sorry, keeping our professional secrets is a matter of deep importance. A matter of *grave* importance, you could say.

RADEK (*expressively*): *Grave* importance! (*Everyone laughs, again*).

YAGODA (*jokingly*): You can be dead sure of that! I'll just say one thing (*enunciates his words exaggeratedly*): if Soviet power still hasn't "put the lid" on us yet, it's because of this achievement of my secret police at the Commissariat of Internal Affairs. (*Again pours himself a glass of burgundy and drinks*).

BUKHARIN: Well yes, everyone already knows mares eat oats.

YAGODA: But Zinoviev and Kamenev didn't understand that, and are only learning now what happens when you turn up your noses at me.

RYKOV: Hyeah, we know all about those bastards!

ZINAIDA (*peeking in from the dining room*): Aha! Genrikh's here too?! (*Enters and greets Yagoda*). Hello sweetie, are you tired? Hungry? (*He kisses her hand*). I can imagine how stressful this trial has been for you! (*To everyone*): Come, come sit down to eat, comrades, you can talk your fill later! We have some nice fattened chicken and a marvelous Pommard. (*Ushers everyone into the dining room*). Quickly, take your seats ... (*Calls out*): Nanny! Serve them now! (*Everyone rushes joyfully into the dining room. Yagoda stops Zinaida at the threshold and, closing the door quietly leads his lover over to the stagelights*).

YAGODA (*handing the briefcase to her*): Hide this somewhere safe. This is what I mentioned.

ZINAIDA (*almost whispering*): The "case" against ... Stalin? Yes? Documents? Photos?

YAGODA (*the alcohol starting to take effect*): Both, plus the drafts of compromising orders.

ZINAIDA (*anxiously*): Has something happened? Does he have something on you?

YAGODA (*wincing*): The hell he does! It's just a precautionary measure for the "transition period". Even if things do go wrong, which they shouldn't, and he aims his guns at me, don't hesitate for a second: Go to the Politburo, to the members of the Presidium, and expose "daring Joe," help me take his place. Do you understand? (*Slapping the briefcase*). I've been collecting these papers for more than ten years.

ZINAIDA (*taking the briefcase out of Yagoda's hands, speaking at the breakneck pace of a conspirator*): Don't worry, my dear: if anything happens, God forbid, you can depend on me, like a ...

VARVARA (*opens the door to the dining room, where we see the nanny walking serving the roasted chicken to each of the guests*): Zina! Why have you gone and abandoned your guests? They want to drink to your health.

ZINAIDA: Just a minute ... (*to Yagoda*): Have you met? My sister, Varvara, I hope you shall get along famously.

YAGODA (*greeting Varvara with the look of a Don Juan*): "Get along"? "Always at the ready," as our Young Pioneers say. As for "famously," you can count on my highest regard. (*Kisses Varvara's hand. To Zinaida*): I had no idea you had such an enchanting little sister!

ZINAIDA (*laughing*): I am happy for my sister and even ... flattered ... Let's take our seats for dinner then, before it gets cold. (*Exits into the dining room, partially closing the door behind her*).

VARVARA (*to Yagoda*): So you are that terrible Chekist, the source of all the legends abroad?

YAGODA (*with refined courtesy*): The rumors are flattering. But ... do I really look like a "bloodsucking vampire"?

VARVARA: Hmmm ... how shall I put it ... are you proud of this nickname?

YAGODA (*seriously*): Drinking the blood of the enemies of the Soviet Union and the oppressors of the proletariat is not such a great crime as you think.

VARVARA: So is it tasty, human blood?

YAGODA: Hmm ... like aged burgundy. (*Turning to the table*): Would you like a glass of this marvelous liquid? (*Pours some for her and for himself*). With a little imagination it can quell the thirst for justice.

VARVARA (*unable to bring herself to drink*): Brrr! Is this ...

YAGODA (*laughing*): You can be dead sure it isn't! This is the best drink in the world. (*She drinks, he laughs*). Does it remind you of blood?

VARVARA: I don't know, but ... you don't seem very much like what I imagined.

YAGODA (*taking her by the hand*): And you, on the other hand, are quite similar to my ideal: zesty and proud, reasonable "sex appeal," with a feline femininity ... well, in a word, an angel of midnight manufactured in Paris.

VARVARA (*laughing*): I see you don't skimp on compliments.

YAGODA (*suggestively*): And it doesn't stop there. You see ... I find you terribly fetching.

VARVARA: "Terribly"? ... Well, then I should stay out of your way.

YAGODA: Banish the thought! Otherwise I might have to "tail" you! Does that frighten you?

ZINAIDA (*throwing the door to the dining room open*): Varya! Genrikh! Come along to dinner! Everyone's waiting for you.

YAGODA AND VARVARA (*simultaneously*): Coming, coming! (*They exit, together with Zinaida, into the dining room, where the feasters greet them with the raised glasses and shouts of "To your health!"*).

Curtain

Second Scene

In Gorki, a suburb of Moscow, at Stalin's residence.

Late evening in the study of the Soviet dictator. Relatively humble dimensions, furnished in a "spartan" manner, illuminated by a large lamp over his desk which shines bright light out from under a dark lampshade.[*]

The light does not eliminate all the darkness from the study—only some of it around the desk, leaving the walls, hung with maps and photographs, in transparent semidarkness, as well as the windows, which are hidden under heavy curtains.

As the curtain rises, the master of the house is seated at the desk close to the stagelights, with his back half-turned towards the audience, displaying his commanding "silhouette" against the bright background cast by the lamp.

Before him, well-illuminated by the same lamp, are Yezhov, standing behind the desk to the left, and Yagoda, sitting in a chair to the right.

Yezhov, Stalin's "faithful policeman" (as he was dubbed in the GPU) presents a perfectly homely figure of a diminutive height standing on crooked, spindly legs. His face, angular and knobby, the size of a fist, with the forehead of a "cretin," is a pale grey color, with piercing little eyes that "bore right through you." His face is bordered by huge saucer-like ears and divided by a thin-lipped, feminine mouth. Yezhov "speechifies" in a high-pitched falsetto, but there's nothing "effeminate" about his voice. Nikolai Ivanovich Yezhov wears the military uniform

---

*   Anatoly Yar-Kravchenko's painting "Gorky Reads to Stalin" gives an impression of what the interior of Stalin's house looked like. It was reproduced in the Soviet magazine *Novyi mir* (1947, no. 11). [Author's footnote.]

of the NKVD, with a bulky revolver on his waistbelt, which lends the finishing touch of caricature to the Soviet Union's noteworthy "bloody dwarf".[76]

The traits of the master himself are more complex. Among the outward features which are conveyed by portraits of Stalin, it is important to note his moderate stature, his bowleggedness (the root of his wide duck-like saunter) and the somewhat lumpy features of his rigid face, giving the impression that it is almost swollen. Iosif Vissarionovich is dressed in a grey "Stalinka," something between a military coat and a soldier's tunic, and black pants tucked into medium-length boots made from soft leather, the kind worn by simple people of the Transcaucasia region. "The first impression" one has of Stalin, as his former secretary B. Bazhanov[77] *writes, "is of a restrained, calm and simple man. At the same time you think he must also be very intelligent".*[78] *But upon a closer acquaintance with the dictator, it becomes apparent that "you are dealing with a man without culture, without an education, who does not know foreign languages or Russian literature or life abroad."*[79] *When one of the participants at a meeting of the Sovnarkom proposed appointing an "efficient and intelligent" candidate as a People's Commissar to the People's Commissariat of the Workers' and Peasants' Inspection, Lenin interrupted him, declaring, "well, we don't need a smart one there; we'll send Stalin ...".*[80] *For the most part, Stalin is clever rather than intelligent, something which one can see in his expression, in his smile and in the intonations of his voice. The guttural tones typical of Transcaucasian highlanders are likewise standard parts of his speech. Stalin's "Eastern" cleverness has also made its mark on the general expression of his face, forming the image of a "genial master," although not too much so, and of a man who "knows what he's worth". What precisely he is "worth" is suggested by his "swinish"—again in the words of B. Bazhanov—attitude towards those who appeared before him in trembling supplication.*[81] *For example, Stalin rings a bell. The messenger girl on duty runs off somewhere and one of his assistants enters the room (Tovstukha or Kanner*[82]*). Stalin utters a single word, "matches," or "tea"! and they run off to carry out the orders of the Soviet satrap.*[83] *"In one and a half years of continuous service to Stalin," B. Bazhanov "did not hear him yell, speak in anger or even raise his voice a single time,"*[84] *not to mention the absence of any superfluous gesticulation, "waving his hands" and suchlike. His calm certainty in the party tactics he follows with the utmost rigor sometimes makes for a kind of hypnosis: it seems as if the crown of a dictator truly rests upon his head, just as real as the pipe of smoldering tobacco he holds in his mouth.*

YAGODA (*continuing with an ongoing discussion*): ... You know very well, Iosif Vissarionovich, how much sweat and craft went into preparing those bastards Zinoviev and Kamenev and their ilk for the court! Here you blame me for the fact that anyone present at the trial could clearly see for themselves that the defendants were not speaking their own words but words forced on them by the authorities, and because of that, you say, all their penitence and self-reproach looked like it was deliberately rigged. And yet, tell me, honestly, could I have allowed this scum to say in court the very things other Oppositionists see as the truth of the "Zinoviev bloc"! Clearly, that would have been pure propaganda against both you and against the whole party, a counter-revolutionary temptation for the whole world! Again, please consider this: I was not the only one preparing the accused, there was also the prosecutor Vyshinsky, and he and I had many differences of opinion. How many things he demanded of the accused, if you only knew! You'd die laughing. And that's just what those weasels wanted, to have to admit to something improbable. Then everyone would have seen it as the result of obvious pressure from the GPU, and not their voluntary confession. If it hadn't been for my energetic protests it would have been such a puppet show that everyone would have split their sides laughing at the trial!

STALIN (*in a dull voice, with a slight regional accent*): And still, they repented as if their words were "sown with white thread"—it was not convincing to anyone! Almost every single member of the Politburo has been calling me on the telephone today since morning: Hwhy did they concoct this ridiculous trial? And furthermore at a time hwhen the members of the presidium are almost all away, Kaganovich[85] is off on assignment, Molotov[86] was not able to warn anybody and you've made such a bungle of it that I do not even know how to respond.

YAGODA: Well, our presidium members are always unhappy about something. Everyone's a critic! …

STALIN: And hhow could they not be critical when the accused exposed themselves in committing fairytale crimes and then even demanded the death sentence for them! It is completely ab-surd: no paper trail, no material evidence, not even a trace of any documents of any kind!

YEZHOV (*deadpan*): That's right! And this is what everyone noticed.

STALIN (*to Yagoda*): It's you who have to understand that that's no way of going about it: a man stands up in court and makes a bald-faced statement that he's committed a crime. So where's the proof? Where's the proof I ask you? Otherwise any man could declare themselves a criminal, if "pressure" is put on him down at Lubyanka.

YAGODA (*nervously, incensed*): So what was I supposed to do, fabricate the documents *myself*?

STALIN: Why *yourself*? What was needed was for the *criminals* to do it … Once a criminal admits to what we need, let him prepare a corresponding document to confirm it.

YAGODA: Well, then it's one and the same: however you spin it, it's a fake!

STALIN: No, it's not the same thing! And as for the "fake," you just forget about that, because what's important is not worrying about your "snow-white robes," but what helps the party and what is required by the dictates of socialist expediency! The party must be monolithic. And if some hacks, out of their own ambition, want to break it up into factions, then they need a sharp slap on the hands! And if that doesn't work, go for the head!

YEZHOV: That's right!

STALIN: It's no time to play nice with the opposition! We are not dealing with a group of people who want to help the party, but with a faction that's lying in wait for the party behind a corner: "Perhaps he will make a mistake, slip up, and then we'll take him out!" It's a faction when they wait for the members of its central institutions in a back alley, to exploit a bad harvest, or a fall in the chervonets,[87] or some other difficulty of the party—and then jump out from behind the corner and bash the party over the head.

YAGODA (*reserved*): I know perfectly well what the faction's moves are about!

STALIN: And if you know, why are you kicking up dust? "A fake" he says … Didn't Lenin teach us that you have to lead the enemy into confusion when you do battle with him? The key thing is what we're fighting for: either it's for the Communist Party, and to keep it monolithic, or against it. And whoever's against it: put them up to "the wall" and shoot them! as Ilich said, end of discussion! When you're at war there's no time to waste on morals, or you're lost!

YEZHOV (*in the bullying tone of a doctrinairian which clearly irks Yagoda*): The Bolshevik Party is not a monastic brotherhood, it's a fighting collective that has one truth—the real one—for internal use, and another—a staged one—for external consumption! Because if you "live with the wolves, you have to howl like one" and everything else needs to be "hush-hush," so "even a bloodhound couldn't sniff it out"!

YAGODA (*fixating on Yezhov with withering scorn*): Where do you get off spouting these nickel-and-dime truisms at me? Decided to give me a lecture, or just showing off your "schooling"?

YEZHOV: Not a lecture, it's a reminder that the stage truth has to have the ring of the real one, otherwise no one will believe it! And if they don't believe it, it's awkward for the whole party and, most of all, for comrade Stalin: didn't see it through, they'll say, couldn't manage to deliver the goods in the right packaging! And then it won't be the people Stalin executes for wrecking and factionalism that they'll consider criminals, it will be Stalin himself: they'll say he's settling personal scores with his former comrades?

YAGODA (*barely restraining his fury*): Listen up, comrade Yezhov! I came here to hear Stalin's opinion, which I take seriously as a party authority. But, excuse me, your oratory does not interest me in the slightest, and I suggest you keep it to yourself.

STALIN (*to Yagoda*): Don't get worked up over trifles! The cause of the party is more important than our personal pride.

YAGODA: Of course, but ... it's surprising to me that Yezhov is present during our discussion.

STALIN: What's surprising about it? Yezhov is the president of the Commission for Party Control and he needs to be kept abreast of developments.

YAGODA: That may be true, but there's no need to teach me how to think!

YEZHOV: And I'm not giving any lessons!

YAGODA (*interrupting him*): First let him serve the party as I've served her these 15 years, and then he can lecture me like some schoolboy!

YEZHOV (*to Stalin*): I can leave if I'm not needed! I came here at your request, Iosif Vissarionovich, and not out of my own desires. (*A muffled ring is heard from the telephone on the table. Yezhov picks up the receiver and says in an icy voice*): Hello! Do you know where you're calling? (*Listens and, covering the receiver, says to Stalin through his teeth*): Radek's arrived … he brought news.

STALIN: Ask: is it something urgent?

YEZHOV (*into the telephone*): Is it urgent? (*Pause. To Stalin*): He says it's urgent.

STALIN: Well fine then! Let him wait a little! I'll call him.

YEZHOV (*into the telephone*): Wait a little, comrade! You'll be called. (*Hangs up the receiver*).

STALIN (*grinning*): He's taking precautions so they don't "set him up" as part of the Zinoviev gang. (*To Yagoda*): By the way: why did you not tell me that Radek, and Bukharin, and Rykov were accessories to the counterrevolutionary intrigues of these rabid dogs?

YAGODA (*icily articulating each word*): Because they do not have anything to do with them. That denunciation was just a bribe to the court which the criminals thought would give them a lighter sentence. (*Screwing up his lips*): Bukharin, Radek and Rykov have been distant from the "rabid dogs" for a long time.[88]

YEZHOV (*squinting*): Well now! I have different information on this question ... I even know who acted as the contact with Bukharin.

STALIN: Who then?

YEZHOV: The terrorist Karev,[89] who was connected to the Kirov murder.[90]

STALIN (*flatly*): It just gets better and better!

YAGODA (*flaring up*): Well, if Yezhov wanted to bring his own personal Cheka to take on the GPU itself—I won't be responsible for what happens to our political investigation!

STALIN (*to him*): Don't overreact, Genrikh! Don't strain yourself! (*To Yezhov*): And you, Nikolai Ivanovich, do us a favor: frisk that Radek before letting him in here. Just do it delicately: like you want to give him a hug. Got it?

YEZHOV (*hesitating*): So we don't have any unpleasantness again, like we had when they frisked Lunacharsky last time?[91]

STALIN: Well that was the former Cultural Commissar, and as harmless as a lamb! But Radek's a different case: A man who called for his former friends to get the death penalty yesterday might try to "execute" the sentence himself today.

YEZHOV (*gloomily troubled*): Better safe than sorry.

STALIN: That's it! If you don't mind!

YEZHOV: Alright! (*Exit*).

STALIN (*stands up and stretches his legs. After a pause*): I wanted to warn you, my dear friend: Some discrepancies came up in your accounting for the Belomor canal.

YAGODA (*unflinching*): I know.

STALIN: Some receipts are missing for certain expenditures. And this gives fodder to venomous tongues, and, how shall I put it, it compromises you.

YAGODA (*going into a rage*): Says who?! Yezhov again? In whose eyes does it compromise me?

STALIN (*smiling*): Shhh! In general, for party supervision … You've grown accustomed to a comfortable life, you occupy a high post, put some holes in quite a few heads without explanation—that's why more is asked of you. And, I don't need to tell you, there are as many people that hate you as me. And many of them are just waiting to throw both of us to the wolves … In other words, I'm warning you … do something about it!

YAGODA (*standing up in fury*): The bastards! They accuse me of embezzlement, when I've saved the state millions with the free labor of prisoners! Enriched the Soviet Union with gigantic works that the Pharaohs of Egypt couldn't even dream of! Made slave labor in the concentration camps so disciplined that we could supply it to state enterprises like a flawless product! And as a thanks for all that I get accused of embezzlement?! They don't even want to slip me a measly pennyworth of a "tip" for everything I've saved us?! Where the hell is the justice in this?

STALIN: Eh, that's what he's after!

YAGODA: Since when did they start calling "savings" "embezzlement"?

STALIN (*looks at the clock, turns on the radio*): Don't ruin your liver! The question is about the formal side of things, and here you are getting emotional.

YAGODA (*catching his breath*): To hell with these ungrateful bastards! If worse comes to worst I can make up for the deficit, if necessary! I hope they choke on my salary, the scum! And they call themselves comrades! Bullshit!

VOICE ON THE RADIO: "… and the heinous gang of Zinoviev, Kamenev, Mrachkovsky,[92] Smirnov[93] and other enemies of the proletariat have finally got what they deserved! The sentence has been carried out! … The air has become cleaner, it's easier to breathe now that this filth has been taken out.

We've received thousands of letters from kolkhoz workers, scientists and writers in the past few days in our red capital. These letters, cast in the millions, express their boundless love for the leader of nations, for the father and the teacher of the toilers, for our dear comrade Stalin. "There is no force in the world," they write in these letters, "that can turn us from Stalin's path. We, the patriots of the Land of the Soviets, stand like an armored wall around the leaders of our party and our government who set the example for this nation of one hundred seventy million! Vigilance and more vigilance—this is what is called for today from every builder of socialism. Look sharp! Don't close your eyes for even a minute! ... Let those who ...[94] (*Stalin, with a smirk, cuts off the radio address. By this time, as the speaker begins to expound upon the "close unity and comradely cohesion of the leaders of the party and the government,"[95] Yezhov has returned and taken his place, in symmetry with Yagoda, standing next to Stalin who has remained in the middle of the room. At the words "boundless love for the leader of nations," "cast in the millions," Stalin begins to laugh sullenly; at the words "close unity and comradely cohesion" of the members of the party and government, all three—Stalin, Yagoda and Yezhov—can barely restrain their mocking laughter*).

YAGODA (*offering his hand to Stalin*): You don't need me here anymore?

STALIN (*shaking his hand*): No, no ... And you won't forget my advice?

YAGODA (*with the maximum degree of warmth available to him*): My dear, to me your advice is the law! (*Offers his hand to Yezhov, coldly*): Bye! Enjoy your stay! (*Exits. Yezhov follows Yagoda to the door and closes it behind him*).

STALIN (*sitting down at the desk again and speaking in a conciliatory tone*): He's ready to top up the funds if there's any deficit there, in the Belamor canal records.

YEZHOV (*with a venomous grin*): "If there's any deficit there"?! Ha, ha. That's not a deficit there, Iosef Vissarionovich, but embezzlement on a scale that's horrid to even imagine!

STALIN (*softly*): Well aren't you snippy! After all, the man made an effort and was even … declared a hero!

YEZHOV: Why he's a regular crook, this self-appointed hero, he's a bandit who should be in the penal colony! A sadist who should be in a noose! A backstabber who doesn't belong in society! And a fraud like him is in charge of the Commissariat of Interior Affairs?! Has control over your personal bodyguards?! Why, it's a *miracle* that no one's knocked you off yet! It's lucky that I was able to get closer to you and expose these bastards that surround you!

STALIN: Oh you really love to lay it on thick, Yezhov! How awful it would be if everything were the way you paint it!

YEZHOV (*squinting his eyes, he pats his briefcase*): Here I have gathered all the information about this.

STALIN (*bleakly*): It's downright horrid to listen to what you're telling me.

YEZHOV: Do you think it isn't horrid for me to tell you about it?

STALIN (*twisting his mouth, after a pause*): So he's aiming at my spot is he?

YEZHOV: You bet he is!

STALIN (*shaking his head*): Idiot! Does he really think he can pull one over on me?

YEZHOV: It's even worse: He thinks he can *disgrace* you in the eyes of the party!

STALIN (*almost yelling*): Yagoda?!

YEZHOV: Him!

STALIN: Bullshit!

YEZHOV: What do you expect from a man who served[96] in the *Tsar's secret police?!*[97] These people won't stop at anything to win themselves a place in the limelight. And Genrikh Yagoda ...

STALIN (*interrupting him*): He was in the Tsar's secret police?!—I don't believe it!

YEZHOV: So what's this then?! (*Takes a police document out of the briefcase and shows it to Stalin: two photos of Yagoda, in profile and en face. Stalin inspects the photos avidly, looks at the document in the light, checks the stamp and signature, flings it on the table with contempt and covers his face with his hand as if in exhaustion*). Satisfied?! I'm not going to lie to you! Now you have seen for yourself that this is a criminal character, from whom we can expect all kinds of surprises. "A mongrel breed of fox and hog,"[98] as Maxim Gorky said about this kind of bastard ... And this Tsarist spy has the audacity to announce, in your presence, that my "oratory" doesn't interest him and I can "keep them to myself"!

STALIN: Eh, toughen up! The time will come for you to settle scores.. I will tell you what I told Dzerzhinsky[99] when he got "offended" (*in a lascivious tone*): "Choose a victim, prepare your strike meticulously, quench your bottomless thirst for revenge and, after that, go to bed. There's nothing sweeter on Earth!"[100] Just have patience!

YEZHOV (*breathing out a long sigh*): Easy to say!

STALIN: Nonsense! "Revenge is a dish best served cold," as they say in Spain. And for now ... Call in that "Robbik,"[101] as they nicknamed him in Poland.

YEZHOV (*starting*): "Robbik"? ... I didn't know Radek had that nickname.

STALIN: Did you frisk that good-for-nothing?

YEZHOV: I embraced him so tenderly, he nearly broke into tears ... (*They both laugh. Yezhov approaches the phero-phone*[102] *and, picking up the receiver, speaks distinctly*): Iosif Vissarionovich awaits comrade Robbik, that is, pah!—Karl Radek. (*Hangs up the receiver. Lowers his voice and pointing furtively at the door*): That son of a bitch is afraid that they'll frame him up with Kamenev and Zinoviev, but the lousy bastard doesn't know that he's already been framed up with Piatakov,[103] Sokolnikov[104] and all that riff-raff.

STALIN (*grinning*): Just like he doesn't know that there's a whole other trial coming to take care of all the red dregs who've come up against me ... (*Almost in a whisper and raising a finger in warning*): But about that quiet ... to everyone! Shhh! ... You hear?

YEZHOV (*shushing and nodding his head in agreement*): Shhh! ... Got it! ... (*Exits, almost on tip-toe, running into Karl Radek at the threshold*).

RADEK (*entering with an affected familiarity*): Long live the invaluable leader of the proletariat! (*Greeting Stalin*): How is your precious health?

STALIN (*shaking his guest's hand*): Here, brother, you shouldn't think about health, but about how to stay alive.

RADEK: And that's precisely why I'm here. (*Greets Yezhov*).

STALIN: Any news? ... Take a seat!

RADEK: Yes! And something unexpected. (*Takes a seat opposite Stalin, brightly lit by the lamp*).

STALIN (*twisting his mouth*): Yet another conspiracy?

RADEK: You guessed it!

STALIN (*grinning*): And of course, first off with the head of "the Father of Nations"?

RADEK (*smiling*): That can't be avoided, since you are, after all, the "head" of the party, Iosif Vissarionovich.

STALIN (*flying into a rage*): God damn it! I have the nerves of an elephant, but even they can't withstand all these schemes, attempts, plots, threats to my life, factional intrigues and ordinary backroom backstabbing.

RADEK: Yes, we haven't had times like this in a long while!

STALIN (*interrupting him, not listening*): Yes, isn't it strange! The more praise I get, the more assassination attempts there are! It's like a joke! ... And why, is it envy? Could anyone really want to put themselves in my shoes?

RADEK: What do you expect of idiots with ambition?

STALIN (*continuing his own thought*): As long as I was the party secretary, no one made any attempts on my life or to slander me. But as soon as I became the "Father of Nations" I can barely even show my face in public! And if they ever declared me to be the Lord God—I wouldn't have a snowball's chance in hell!

RADEK (*laughing*): ... You wouldn't last through the day!

STALIN: I think so, too.

RADEK: After all, God isn't something to be sneezed at!

STALIN: Fools! (*Sighing*): Well, tell me, who else is out there conspiring?.. And most importantly: Are these rumors, or facts?

RADEK: Facts, facts! And they are urgent! I rushed to you at full steam!

STALIN: What is it?

RADEK (*looks over his shoulder at the door and blurts out*): Tukhachevsky!

STALIN (*dumbfounded*): What about "Tukhachevsky"?

RADEK: Marshall Tukhachevsky!

STALIN: Marshall Tukhachevsky?

RADEK: Precisely!

STALIN (*reflecting*): Hmm ... I know about him!

RADEK (*with a smile*): Well who doesn't know about him!

STALIN (*severely*): No wisecracking when talking about serious business! ... (*Restrained*): I've already received reports about him ... Who else is with him?

RADEK (*looking around*): Gamarnik, Yakir, Uborevich and Kork.[105] A big military plot.

STALIN: These aren't rumors?

RADEK: Not at all!

STALIN: Prove it!

RADEK: Tukhachevsky is looking for support among right-leaning party members.

STALIN: For example?

RADEK: Hmm. Bukharin.

STALIN: Liar!

RADEK: But I'm not lying! He needs to recruit bigwigs among Lenin's former companions.

STALIN: Yeah right, Bukharin laughs at him, calls him "Little Napoleon".

RADEK: Bukharin isn't cozying up to Tukhachevsky, it's the other way around, Tukhachevsky's idea.

STALIN: Prove it!

RADEK: It's quite simple! (*Lights his pipe*). A few days ago I rang at Bukharin's: Is Marshal Tukhachevsky there? "No," answered a female voice, "he's not expected today ..." Aha! I thought, he's not expected today, but generally, he is!

STALIN: Well, that's weak!

RADEK: I know, that's why I tried to confirm it!

STALIN: And?

RADEK: I did! (*Takes a drag from the pipe*).

STALIN: And what exactly?

RADEK: Yesterday I was telling Bukharin a joke ... I hadn't told anyone this joke of mine before him, except ... except Marshall Tukhachevsky, who, as you well know, likes to get by on other people's wit.

STALIN: So what?

RADEK: Bukharin wouldn't let me finish: "I've heard this little joke," he says, "don't you have anything fresh? ..." Aha! I think, gotcha!

STALIN: Who? Bukharin?

RADEK: Tukhachevsky! It must mean that he meets with Bukharin, cozies up to him, and to ingratiate himself with Bukharin, he tells him fresh little jokes.

STALIN (*smirking*): Well, look at you, provocateur!

RADEK: And what are you supposed to do with these military people, when they are so conspiratorial that one brother won't tell the other what his mom and pop call him at home.

STALIN: And so what is this "Napoleon" scheming at?

RADEK: Actually, sorry, I don't call him "Napoleon," I call him "Howlongseon".

STALIN: What's that mean?

RADEK: "Howlongseon"? It means "how long" will "he" be able to go on thinking he's a genius?

STALIN (*laughing*): Aha! It took me a second.

RADEK: It's unprecedented arrogance: He wants to raise an army against the Kremlin, remove you from power, take your place and end the Communist Party.

STALIN: Ah yes ... This business is nonsense! What kind of slogan is this "Howlongseon" of yours going to use to launch his campaign?

RADEK: (*ironically*): A patriotic one!

STALIN (*shocked*): A patriotic one?

RADEK: A patriotic one! He claims that settling the kolkhozes, and exiling people to Siberia if they were dissatisfied, including confiscating all their possessions, resulted in *famine*, even in the best bread-basket regions. Millions of peasants, says he, fled from disaster to the cities. And when rumors spread about an imminent German invasion, the Germans weren't seen as enemies of our homeland, but as rescuers from your disastrous experiments.

STALIN: "Disastrous"?

RADEK (*unctuously*): Not my words: That's what they say!

STALIN (*angry*): Who?

RADEK: Tukhachevsky and them!

STALIN: Go on!

RADEK: They were claiming that, whatever happens, it couldn't get any worse: "the krauts can't do any more harm to our homeland than Stalin!"

STALIN (*purple with rage*): "Harm"?

RADEK: Again, not my words, that's what the military conspirators say!

STALIN: Well what else? What a bunch of hogwash!

RADEK: With this defeatist perspective, the military leadership has no doubt at all that the Soviet Union will be utterly crushed on the field of battle. And so, in order to avert it, Tukhachevsky and other commanders cooked up a political coup: We need to reject the "Stalin regime," they say, give everyone faith in tomorrow, and... emancipate the peasants.

STALIN: "Emancipate"?!

RADEK: And the "miraculous Georgian,"[106] that is you, Iosif Vissarionovich, must be ejected from here through the wall of the Kremlin.

STALIN (*grinning*): "The miraculous Georgian"!... Oh c'mon Tukhachevsky! And this man has a marshal's staff! Well then, look what we've come to ... So is there any way to avoid executions here? Teach me!

RADEK: It's absolutely crucial in your position! Jokes aside, Descartes taught that "cogito, ergo sum," i.e. "I think, therefore I am". But your existence, as the head of the government, follows exclusively from executions: You exist, because you execute! And, vice versa: You shoot, therefore you are! It's as clear as two plus two!

STALIN: You can't do without the sophistry, can you? But I'm starting to think you were right when you insisted, at the start of the revolution, that all its traitors be shot *in public*.[107] (*Pause*): What else does he accuse me of, your "Howlongseon"?

RADEK (*furrows his brow*): Well ... quite a lot! I'd feel bad repeating all of it: I'm not a gossip!

STALIN: Don't you be shy! An ass might bray, but they don't hear it in heaven!

RADEK (*the more he smokes, the more he feels "at home" and loosens up in his criticisms, served in the form of denunciations*): Well, he charges that we have a political regime of irresponsible dictatorship in which an armed minority rides roughshod over a disarmed majority.

STALIN: Yes, yes! ...

RADEK: He says that there's no country where the workers live in worse conditions than in the USSR or where they are exploited so barbarously.

STALIN: Yes, yes! ...

RADEK: He claims that we've reduced the Communist Party to a *primitive, wretched condition* perhaps only comparable to Eskimos, who used to have a rich, cultured life ...

STALIN (*raising his eyebrows*): "Eskimos"? ... Who was it that was telling me about Eskimos? Ah, yes, Demian Bedny!

RADEK (*flaring up*): Plagiarist!

STALIN: Only he claims that this was your invention.

RADEK (*blushing*): Mine?! (*Grinning*): Hmm ... that is about as true as saying that "poor" Demian Bedny,[108] who is subsidized by our state treasury, is actually as poor as his name says.

STALIN: Fine! The hell with Demian! I want to know what Tukhachevsky is saying.

RADEK (*regaining his self-control, he continues with a sarcasm that takes on a more and more ambivalent quality*): Tukhachevsky, by the way, swears that the resolution on the new constitution[109] which you are so proud of was not passed by the Politburo with your help, but actually *in opposition* to you and your wishes.

STALIN: How's that?

RADEK: That they wanted to use the constitution to limit your dictatorship! But that you, having understood their ploy, declared that you were the author of the constitution in order to then have all the "constitutionalists" shot.[110]

STALIN (*smiles amiably and shakes his head*): What a piece of scum he takes me for!

RADEK: And not only him, honest!

STALIN (*interrupting him, almost barking*): What?

RADEK: Nothing! You wanted me to be honest, so there you have it!

STALIN (*interrupting*): I only wanted to know what Tukhachevsky's been saying! But I don't give a damn about the others in the slightest and I wouldn't hesitate to have the entire Central Committee shot if I have to! Got that?

RADEK (*hitting his stride in "telling it straight" directly to the dictator he hates*): I know that! And Marshal Tukhachevsky knows it! That's why he doesn't compare your regime to the despots of Asia that don't allow for any kind of authority, even that which they create themselves.

STALIN: Hmm ... Well so what do you say about all this?

RADEK: Me? ... I think these opinions are based on gossip.

STALIN (*impenetrable*): What gossip is being spread about me?

RADEK: All kinds! I'd feel rather bad repeating it.

STALIN: Well, for example?

RADEK: Well, for example: How could a man ruling over one hundred and seventy million citizens care about nonsense like ... gossip!

STALIN: Yes, yes! ...

RADEK: You would have to be an extremely limited person, petty and uncultured, to attribute such an exclusive importance to various rumors about yourself! You would have be a virtual nonentity, a numbskull, to ...

STALIN: Wait a minute! *Who* said that? ... I lost track, is that what Tukhachevsky says or what you are saying?

RADEK (*catching himself*): Him, him! Only "Howlongseon" would allow himself to say such remarks about the brilliant Stalin!

STALIN: And yet *you* allow yourself to *circulate* this bilge with such relish that I can't believe I can stand hearing it!

RADEK (*lost*): Forgive me, Iosif Vissarionovich, I thought it would please you to hear what others are saying about you!

STALIN: Hear how they insult me?! No, brother, don't be sly! If there's somebody who likes this spineless *nitpicking*, that's not me, of course, but you!

RADEK: You're being hard on me, Iosif Vissarionovich! I wanted to please you.

STALIN (*grinning*): Look here, Radek! I'm not a man who stays in debt: Here's a joke for yours. (*After a short pause*): They say that there's only *one* way to earn money *honestly* ...

RADEK (*hardly waiting a second*): And which way is that?

STALIN (*genuinely laughing*): I knew that you didn't know how to do it *that way*!

RADEK (*nonplussed*): Sorry, I ... didn't understand at first. You're saying that ...

STALIN (*cheerful*): ... that there's only *one* way to make money *honestly*. And you asked, which way is that? So you don't know how.

RADEK (*feigned laughter*): Aa! That's it is it! Well now, well done! You got me, no use denying it!

STALIN: You see, I also know how to take the piss. You're not the only one ... And he who laughs last, laughs best! Isn't that right?

RADEK: The sacred truth!

STALIN (*offering his hand, laughing*): Are we done here?

RADEK (*shaking his hand*): Absolutely!

Curtain

(First Intermission)

Third Scene

A small chemical laboratory of the OGPU, in a place called "Sixth Hills". The laboratory is equipped with all the latest technology of 1936 in the field of pharmacology.

The morning sun reflects merrily on every imaginable kind of bulb, retort, boiler, filter, exhaust "screen" and copper tank.

On the left-hand side, close to the stage lights, there is a table with a telephone, a pharmacist's scale, a chronometer, a calendar and writing utensils. Behind this, against the wall, is a comfortable leather armchair; in front of the table there are two chairs. To the right, a bit further from the stage lights, is a table for experiments with laboratory equipment.

Directly in front of the viewer are two windows, high and wide, which show an expansive view of the Kremlin in the distance, basking in the morning light.

The only door, in the background on the right, leads into a blind corridor.

At curtain-up, two people are standing at the "experiment table," leaning over two boxes half-encased in glass: Bulanov, Yagoda's personal secretary, and the lab assistant. The first one is a well-shaven type, muscular but plain, and looks to be a bit over forty years old; the second has quite poor vision, is around thirty years old, wears steel-rimmed glasses and has blond hair, a pimply complexion and is somewhat gangly. Both are dressed in canvas work robes with gas masks, of a prewar type, hanging on bands under their chins.

Bulanov is examining the record apparently handed to him by the lab assistant.

After two or three seconds, from the left, the "famous" doctor Levin, the senior Kremlin doctor, walks in with his uncertain and elderly gait. This "spineless intellectual," an old, non-party, gutless doctor with "an inclination to panic," as Levin was described by his defender, comrade Braude,[111] at the trial of the anti-Soviet bloc.

DR. LEVIN (*greeting Bulanov and the lab assistant*): Well, how is everything?

BULANOV: Couldn't be better: Both the rats and the guinea pigs died in wonderful condition, i.e. no spasms, no bloody foam at the mouth or any other undesired symptoms.

DR. LEVIN (*rubbing his hands together*): Excellent! And when was this? (*Opens the lids of the containers and takes a few steps back*). Uffgh, what a smell … it's strong!

BULANOV (*smiling*): Yes well about that, doctor, excuse the stench please! We had to do all our work in gas masks … (*Takes off his mask and hangs it on the wall, setting the example for the lab assistant*).

DR. LEVIN: And when did the animals die?

BULANOV (*pulling a rat out of one of the boxes by its tail*): The rats died after three hours, and the guinea pigs (*pointing at another box*) a little later. (*The lab assistant hands the notes to Bulanov, who turns them over to Dr. Levin*).

DR. LEVIN (*examines the notes*): Well, well, well! … And you're certain that the animals didn't actually touch the poison?

BULANOV: Absolutely!

DR. LEVIN: You're certain that they only inhaled the poison into their lungs?

BULANOV: Well, naturally! Since the rag with the poison was hung right below the lid, how could the animals even reach it?

DR. LEVIN (*handing back the notes*): You're right. I asked just in case—all kinds of lapses occur.

BULANOV: Well, you know, Genrikh Grigoryevich is so strict with us about this that we don't allow any "lapses" to take place here. And really, if someone wanted to take a man out "quietly," it probably wouldn't leave the slightest trace!

DR. LEVIN (*cleaning his glasses out of discomfort*): Yes, certainly! ... In this respect he's quite a pedant.

BULANOV (*catching Levin's troubled look at the lab assistant, he turns abruptly to him and reproaches him*): What are you doing there sitting on your hands? Eh? Did you get out the Pasteur filters already? Where did you put them?

LAB ASSISTANT: What filters?

BULANOV (*aping him*): "What filters"! No. 3. Go down and check with the orderly.

LAB ASSISTANT: Just a second! (*Runs to the door*).

BULANOV (*persuasively*): Don't just take a second, go find out the details.

LAB ASSISTANT: Yes sir! (*He leaves*).

DR. LEVIN: What filters are those? I forget.

BULANOV: An arbitrary term designating that whoever doesn't need to be in the room should scram.

DR. LEVIN: Ah! I completely forgot.

BULANOV: You see, the lab technician is ill, and his assistant here ... God knows what he has on his mind! (*Enter Yagoda, in an excellent mood*).

YAGODA: Hello, comrades! (*He shakes hands with them*). What weather we have! Just fine! (*To Levin, as he approaches the box with the dead rodents*). Well, how'd it go? How's that mercury you oxidized?

DR. LEVIN: The results are fantastic! (*Bulanov hands the notes to Yagoda*).

YAGODA (*examines the notes*): Wonderful! Now we have to try it on a human organism! (*To Bulanov*): Who's looking lively over there on "death row"? Can you select someone?

BULANOV: Not worth it, Genrikh Grigoryevich: Our lab technician breathed his fill of it and already took to bed; we spoke on the telephone, but he's quite bad, he hardly came to.

YAGODA (*rubbing his hands together*): Well if it's bad, that's good! ... (*Catching himself*): I mean, we've found a reliable drug! (*Shaking Levin's hand*). It's curtains for the "Bloody Dwarf"! ... (*Striding*). A curtain call to the grave for the "ever-watchful eye of the GPU!" Farewell, esteemed comrade Yezhov! (*chuckles*).

DR. LEVIN (*cleaning his glasses out of discomfort*): I'm very glad you're satisfied! It was not an easy task ...

YAGODA: My only request, Lev Grigoryevich, is that you *personally* make sure that all the rugs in Yezhov's office, all the portières, the upholstery, any fabric on the table, the curtains and every other scrap of cloth be soaked in the "full dose" of this liquid, the "*quantum satis*,"[112] as you might say.

DR. LEVIN: And I would actually prefer that "this cup pass me by". Just appearing at Yezhov's office, since he knows how loyal I am to you and does not care for me, would be ... (*Turns toward Bulanov*).

YAGODA: Nonsense! After all we're not talking about going to his current apartment! It's his working office, which he still hasn't moved into.

DR. LEVIN: It doesn't matter, don't you understand, I'm already an old man! Poisoning Gorky and Menzhinsky[113] has already shattered my organism and poisoned my life.

YAGODA (*laughing*): Well that's clever: While poisoning others, you poison yourself. That's a good joke there! (*Looks at Bulanov as he takes out his watch*): You're not in a hurry?

BULANOV: Not at all! You don't need me for the time being?

YAGODA: Would you please?

BULANOV: Yes sir! (*Exit*).

DR. LEVIN: Oh Lord, Genrikh Grigoryevich, these "medical executions" are something thoroughly exacting for a man unused to it!

YAGODA: Hogwash! You should be ashamed to whimper like this! (*Walks up to the desk*).

DR. LEVIN: Forgive me, Genrikh Grigoryevich, but we doctors of the old school were trained, pardon me, to cure people, not to do the opposite! And I'm simply, I repeat, not used to this!

YAGODA (*sitting down in the chair, he squints, showering Dr. Levin with contempt*): You're not used to it? What is it that you're not used to? Not used to killing our mutual enemies?

DR. LEVIN (*mumbling*): By God, I'm not used to it!

YAGODA (*jeering cruelly*): Getting a dacha out of me as a gift, you're used to that are you? Fine wines, cigars, golden cigarette cases—all that you can stomach?[114] But when it's time to dispose of the enemies of the people, then it turns out that you aren't used to it? ... And this is after you've killed a whole string of our party officials?

DR. LEVIN: I did that while gritting my teeth ... To be useful to you.

YAGODA: But not for my personal benefit?! You knew perfectly well that I'm only the mouthpiece for the comrades who decided to replace the leaders of our party politics because of the general dissatisfaction with them.

DR. LEVIN: Pardon me, but was Maxim Gorky really a member of the Politburo?

YAGODA: No, but ... who defended Stalin's idiotic policies more than anyone, if not Gorky?

DR. LEVIN: "Idiotic"?!

YAGODA: How else would you describe creating socialism in one *single* country? In the same way you could create socialism in one *single* district, or even a single back alley! It's for good reason that Radek mentioned Shchedrin-Saltykov[115] and his idiot administrator who introduced liberalism in just a *single* district.[116]

DR. LEVIN (*mumbling*): Yes, but if it was Stalin who made mistakes then ...

YAGODA (*finishing his sentence*): ... then Gorky shouldn't have defended him! And you know how much the opinion of this complete and utter "Stalinist" counted! "Gorky said this," "Gorky believes that," "Gorky thinks this is right, and he thinks that is wrong" ... (*Spits bitterly*): Pah, God damn it! Just like the Pope ... And all Stalin needed was for this "infallible" authority, this hypocrite, to defend him, may he be triple damned!

DR. LEVIN (*throwing up his hands*): How can you say this about Gorky, when he praised you as a hero for the Belomor canal!

YAGODA: I don't give a damn about forced compliments! Gorky wasn't lavishing those on me, they were for Stalin's benefit, when Stalin was cowering behind me like a child behind his nanny. But you can be dead sure about one thing! (*Stands up and walks around*): You didn't just do away with those men for my benefit, it was for the benefit of our enslaved motherland, which had a *bitter* life under comrade Gorky the *Bitter's* protectorate,[117] and finally people like Bukharin, Rykov and I decided to free our motherland from her *bitter* fate.

DR. LEVIN: Pardon me, but what about the murder of Gorky's son?

YAGODA: Max?[118]

DR. LEVIN: Yes. For his wife, who you were pursuing openly?[119] ... (*Yagoda waves him away with a tired smile*). And poisoning that engineer Popov in the hospital, the husband of your current mistress Zinaida Avdeevna?! Was that also something I didn't do for your benefit but for the benefit of our "enslaved motherland"?

YAGODA (*angry, looking at the clock*): Well if you start counting every dropped stitch then we'll never get anywhere! And anyways, there's no time for it: Yezhov will move into his office any day now and then ... we won't have a snowball's chance in hell!

LAB ASSISTANT (*entering*): The "Pasteur filters" still haven't arrived, so ...

YAGODA: What are you doing bursting in here like a wild animal?!

LAB ASSISTANT: And so the "Pasteur filters" ...

YAGODA: I heard! Go and call the central warehouse on Miasnitskaia: "When will you have it?" (*Seeing that the lab assistant is heading for the telephone on the table*): Where in hell are you going? That telephone is special-use only! Go up to the main office! (*He runs off. Speaking to Dr. Levin, coming up close to him*): This is the situation: Yezhov is learning all the details about our work in the Directorate of State Security incredibly quickly, and I really cannot say with any certainty whether the "Bloody Dwarf" has already figured out all the pieces of our plot against Stalin. And if that's true, then it's time for both of us to dig our own graves!

DR. LEVIN: You shouldn't say that! You can't be sure!

YAGODA: You can be dead sure of it! And this is why you should stop being an ass and do what I tell you! I want him to be poisoned according to all the laws of science! And you have a good head for science and I respect it!

DR. LEVIN: But my nerves might fail me. I'm 67 years old ...

YAGODA (*shifting his tone*): You should be more worried about *my* nerves ... because, if you leave me in the lurch for this murder, I will think up an end for you that would make Malyuta Skuratov[120] spin in his grave!

DR. LEVIN: But what if I don't have the strength?

YAGODA: Bullshit! You weren't afraid to send Gorky off to the next life, but now with Yezhov you got scared?! Is that right?! More afraid of that than me, who only has to whistle and all that will be left of you is a scrap of putrid sludge! (*A "coded" knock is heard at the door*). Come in!

BULANOV (*entering*): Citizen Descourcel has arrived at your personal invitation.

YAGODA (*rejoicing*): Ahh, yes! About some rigamarole with customs ... Have her come here ... Is it true that she's quite enchanting?

BULANOV (*breaking into a grin*): Extremely.

YAGODA: Your taste isn't bad. (*Stopping him as he moves toward the door*): Wait! (*To Dr. Levin*): By the way this would be a good guinea pig, we can test out that "Veritophor" on her ... Have you figured out the dosage?

DR. LEVIN (*confused*): "Veritophor"?

YAGODA: Yes, the "truth serum" that David Surok[121] invented. (*To Bulanov*): Go sterilize a syringe, quickly.

DR. LEVIN (*understanding*): Ah! The Veritophor! (*Chuckling*). From the word "veritas," which means "truth"? (*Bulanov, who has stepped over to the experiment table, lights a burner under a small water tank and places a syringe in the water*).

YAGODA (*impatient*): What dose do you need for a healthy organism?

DR. LEVIN: To loosen the subject's tongue? Hmm ... half a syringe to paralyze the "control centers"; a whole syringe for maximum release ... (*Takes a small vial from the shelf*). I concentrated the liquid as you requested, and now the effect is achieved in two minutes. (*Hands the vial to Yagoda*).

YAGODA: And how long does it last?

DR. LEVIN: Hmm ... no more than about ten minutes.

YAGODA (*rubbing his hands*): Excellent … (*To Bulanov*): Call in citizen Descourcel. (*Exit Bulanov. To Dr. Levin*): And you sit here in the library for now and let that sink into your brain, what I told you about Yezhov. Just think what a sigh of relief we will breathe when this "shit in the grass" is off of our path!

DR. LEVIN (*in a whining tone*): But I've prepared the poison we need already, what else do you want from me? Can't you have someone else spray Yezhov's office?

YAGODA (*sputtering*): And what if he doesn't inhale enough of this poison to die, eh? What if the dog doesn't kick the bucket? What then? Just accept the existence of this bastard, when our own lives depend it?! (*A knock at the door. Silence*). Wait for me for now, and then we will discuss what to do. This is a matter of life and death, not for commissar Yezhov, but for us! Do you understand? (*Sitting down at the desk, he barks at the door*): Who is it? Come it. (*Enter Bulanov, who ushers in Varvara Descourcel, who is dressed modestly but elegantly. Dr. Levin edges over to the door*). Aah! Varvara Avdeevna? What a pleasure to see you! Please take a seat! (*Points toward the chair in front of his desk. Dr. Levin disappears, almost on tiptoe, closing the door behind him, while Bulanov returns to the boiler with the syringe*).

VARVARA (*sitting down in the chair*): Excuse me, but what have I got myself into here? I was called in about some trivial customs problem with some books I brought my sister from Paris, and this seems to be some kind of laboratory, if I'm not mistaken?

YAGODA: That's right, this is the lab of the OGPU. I didn't want to call you in to the Lubyanka and make any unnecessary noise. Besides, I also have an emulsion I need to investigate here.

VARVARA (*in a genteel tone*): Oh Lord, no need to make excuses, I know how busy you are!

YAGODA (*almost laughing*): Hmm ... It's you who will need to "make excuses" my dear, not me! Because among your books they found a proclamation which you, apparently, were planning to distribute! ... (*Takes a folder out of the desk drawer, and, from the folder, a printed flyer*).

VARVARA (*gasping*): A "proclamation"?! I didn't have any kind of "proclamation"! They obviously slipped that on me!

YAGODA (*ironically*): "Slipped"? To ruin you, of course, for "living the good life" and to receive in exchange the approval of their superiors?

VARVARA: Perhaps.

YAGODA: No, citizen, the officers of the GPU have far too little time to waste on trifles! And the matter presents itself in a completely different light if one bears in mind that you are a foreign national and that your husband is a public figure who is hostile to the "Popular Front"[122] which we support in both France and Spain ... (*Reads the "proclamation"*): "Soviet rule has given millions upon millions of peasants nothing but poverty, hunger and slavish dependence on the collective farm bosses. Workers stand in lines for their daily bread and throng around the employment office, hoping that the Communist bosses have mercy on them and employ them". (*With a chuckle*): And so on, in the same vein? (*Staring at Varvara*): Don't you know this text? Is this the first time you've heard it?

VARVARA: I repeat—I did not have any "proclamation" among the books, and, in general, I do not get involved in such things!

YAGODA (*with murderous irony*): Really?! And you haven't flapped your mouth, haven't said anything in the spirit of this proclamation about our system of government? About

Stalin? About the GPU, in whose laboratory you currently find yourself?

VARVARA (*regaining control of herself*): I don't at all "flap my mouth" as you put it!

YAGODA (*calling*): Comrade Bulanov, come here for a moment! (*Bulanov approaches the table. Yagoda scribbles a few words on his notepad and, tearing off the page, hands it to Bulanov*): Please bring this person here.

BULANOV: Yes sir! (*Exit*).

YAGODA: If you are going to make such sweeping criticisms of all the state structures of the Soviet Union, it will not only mean trouble for you—there will also be trouble for your sister as well as for me, since I am bound to her as a friend!

VARVARA: I am not afraid for myself: after all, I am a foreign national! But for Zina ...

YAGODA (*interrupting*): No ambassador can save you if I have you imprisoned in a basement for ... espionage!

VARVARA: For "espionage"?!

YAGODA: Yes! Are you surprised?! And yet, there is enough evidence for it! I hope you understand how it looks? ... So I think that we had better become friends!

VARVARA (*slightly mockingly*): And what exactly do you mean by "friends"?

YAGODA: First of all, honesty! Being completely honest with one another. Not being secretive, as you are now!

VARVARA: But what am I hiding from you?! Why are you hounding me?

YAGODA (*laughing*): I warned you from the very beginning that I would "hound" you!

VARVARA: You make such sweet jokes! But ... really, is it actually necessary to praise everything in the Soviet regime without exception?

YAGODA: Oh, no one requires that you do so! But to exclaim that Russia is run by Jews who destroy churches for the glory of the Jewish nation ...That means you are setting the dark masses against the most glorious leaders of the USSR!

VARVARA: But I've heard that you are struggling against these leaders yourself, together with uncle Bukharin, Rykov and others.

YAGODA: That is a special case! We are fighting against the usurpers of Soviet power, not with the true leaders of the proletariat! (*There is a knock at the door*): Come in. (*Enter Bulanov, followed by Nanny Zakharovna of the Popova household*).

VARVARA (*seeing Zakharovna*): Nanny! What in the world has brought you here?! And I was worried this morning, wondering where you were! I thought you had taken permission from Zina to go to church.

NANNY (*waving her hand*): What church! I go to "check in" at the GPU! I am a supervised woman, after all, from a concentration camp!

VARVARA: Oh, is that what it is? A "check in"!

NANNY: Usually I always go to the Lubyanka, but for some reason it was here today. (*Bulanov returns to the experiment table, where the syringe is being sterilized.*)

YAGODA (*to her*): Tell me, nanny: I am in a little dispute with Varvara Avdeevna. Is it right for her to rail against the Soviet regime from all the rooftops?

NANNY (*with disarming simplicity*): Well, how can she not? She has cause, Genrikh Grigorievich. Because what kind of "regime" is this anyways? It's a regime of penny-pinching, don't you know it. It's not a regime, it's an extortion ring! They're putting the squeeze on us, and folks can't breathe! (*General laughter*).

YAGODA: Well, and what about the Jews, how does she relate to them? (*Nods toward Varvara*).

NANNY: Varvara Avdeevna?.. Well not at all: She's not at all a Jew.

YAGODA: I know that ... But how does she relate to them?

NANNY: She doesn't relate to them at all: She's orthodox and relates to orthodox folk, not to Jews.

YAGODA: That's correct. But I wonder what she says about Jews and about me in particular?

NANNY: Well, as you know, there's not a good word to be said about Jews, since they're not baptized! And as for yourself, you may ask her that very well on your own. Because a woman's heart, that's something no one can unravel. (*General laughter*).

YAGODA (*cheering up*): That's very well, but what did she say about me to her sister?

NANNY: She laughed at you, just like you laughed at me. She said that she would never take a man like yourself for a lover, and that she thought you were a hangman, pardon me sir, and that she, as it were, doesn't care for hangmen.

YAGODA (*laughs. To Varvara*): Oh, is that how it is? (*To Nanny*): So hangmen don't suit her do they? That's what we'll write down then!

NANNY: Oh, how I praised you for your angelic heart, for letting me out of the concentration camp! And Varvara Avdeevna insisted: He's a hangman, says she, and the whole regime in Russia is of hard labor, may it be damned to hell!

YAGODA (*sighing*): Well, thank you, nanny, for your righteous words! Go home, I don't need anything more from you today.

NANNY (*bowing*): Good day, Genrikh Grigorievich, keep me, poor sinner, in your good graces! (*To Varvara*): Goodbye,

Varvara Avdeevna! Don't linger here, or you'll be late for breakfast! (*Exit to general laughter*).

YAGODA (*to Varvara*): Well, you are quite the secretive lady, Varvara Avdeevna! I never expected that from you. You certainly can't judge a book by its cover. But here we prefer the ones who wear their heart on a sleeve, who are as trusting as children and hide nothing from us.

VARVARA (*at a loss*): But ... I hardly know you! ...

YAGODA: That is no excuse! You are confusing this interrogation with a high-society conversation. And these are two big differences, as they say in Odessa ... And since you were intentionally disingenuous in your testimony, would you allow me, in order to help you atone for your guilt, to test a serum on you that ... will give you the courage to tell the truth?

VARVARA (*turning pale*): And ... what is it exactly? Some kind of torture you've devised?

YAGODA (*almost laughing*): Oh, no! Who speaks of "torture" in our enlightened age ... (*Shaking a bottle of Veritophor, which he placed on the desk earlier*). It is just a special injection, called Veritophor. (*Stands up*).

VARVARA (*barely restraining her irony*): And so you need my permission?! (*Stands up, taking a few steps back from Yagoda at the same time as Bulanov appears directly behind her*).

YAGODA (*grabbing her firmly by the hands*): No, but, as a gentleman, I prefer to touch ladies with their consent.

VARVARA (*wincing, attempts to free her hands from Yagoda's grip*): You're hurting me! Let me go!

YAGODA (*making a sign to Bulanov, who immediately takes out a pair of the handcuffs which modern police forces use to "paralyze" criminals*): There's no need to be anxious, Varvara Avdeevna, it won't help anything! (*Bulanov quickly and skill-*

fully slips the handcuffs on her wrists, after which Yagoda releases her hands and, with cold-bloodedness calculated for full effect, takes a syringe from the "experiment table").

VARVARA (*bewildered*): I don't understand, is this one of your jokes or ...

LAB ASSISTANT (*rushing in, slightly in a sweat*): The Pasteur filters won't be delivered here until 6pm.

YAGODA (*to him, in a rude and threatening tone*): And you'll be delivered to the Lubyanka even sooner than that, if you break in here again without knocking! (*Fills a syringe with Veritophor serum*).

BULANOV (*to the lab assistant*): Go to the depot on Myasnits-kaya! Do you hear? You're not needed here.

LAB ASSISTANT (*stammering*): Myasnitskaya? Yes, sir! (*He disappears. Bulanov locks the door behind him.*)

YAGODA (*to Bulanov*): Help me! (*Bulanov runs up to him and rolls up Varvara's sleeve*).

VARVARA (*indignant*): But, after all, this is completely unheard-of violence! What right do you have?! How dare you?!

YAGODA (*coldly, enunciating his words precisely*): It's my duty, madam! And I'll have you know, the officers of State Security have no regard for bourgeois prejudices! (*He plunges the syringe into her arm, while Bulanov holds her arms*).

VARVARA (*cries out*): Ow!

YAGODA: Hurts, does it? What an actress you are! (*Varvara, lifting her shoulders in indignation, steps away to the window and looks dejectedly at the Kremlin in the distance. Yagoda grumbles, turning to Bulanov*): How can we make sure this fool doesn't bungle things up on Myasnitskaya? Maybe you should call ahead about those Pasteur filters?

BULANOV (*barely restraining a smile*): I serve with pleasure! (*Exit. Distant sound of the Kremlin clock striking noon. Yagoda approaches Varvara and tries to embrace her*).

VARVARA (*avoiding his touch*): Why are you doing all this?

YAGODA: Don't you understand how much I like you?

VARVARA: So what is this then? (*Indicates her handcuffs*): Is this how you win a woman's heart?

YAGODA (*laughing*): Every man does it in his own way. My lot is to woo women as a Chekist. Take me as I am!

VARVARA: Thank you very much, but… First of all, I'm married.

YAGODA: I know! Your husband is 53 years old.

VARVARA: … and, second, even if I weren't married, even then …

YAGODA: … you wouldn't stoop to be with a Chekist? Is that what you want to say?

VARVARA: More or less!

YAGODA: And why is that, if I may ask?

VARVARA: Because a Chekist is the same thing as a hangman, and maybe even worse.

YAGODA: Is that what you think?

VARVARA: What's the difference then? They're almost indistinguishable!

YAGODA (*laughing*): Thank you for your honesty! I love honesty, and I hate hypocrisy, which is imposed on us by our upbringing, political calculations, selfish considerations! (*Looking at the clock*): The Veritophor should have already taken effect! Be completely honest with me. Don't be afraid to be sincere!

VARVARA (*defiantly*): I'm not afraid of anything!

YAGODA: Here's a brave one! I love brave girls! (*Approaching the box of rats*): And you're also not afraid of rats? (*Pulls a rat out by its tail and swings it in front of Varvara's nose*): Not afraid of rats? (*Varvara shrieks hysterically and starts weeping loudly, turning away to the window. Yagoda throws the rat into the box*). So brave! Ay-ay-ay, your nerves are shot! Crying as if she'd been abused!

VARVARA: Let me go home! Do you hear me? Get my hands out of these things! Right now! I am a free citizen of France, not a Soviet slave! What a disgrace to humiliate a defenseless woman like this!

YAGODA: Wow, what a tone she's taken! (*Looking at his watch*): That's the Veritophor starting to do its work!

VARVARA: Let me go! Immediately! (*Sobs silently. Her last words are interrupted by the telephone ringing*).

YAGODA (*picking up the receiver*): Hello ... Oh, is that you, Brik?[123] Hello, Osip. What ...? You can't interrogate archpriest Zavadsky?[124] Why not? They overcooked the bastard in the hot cell? Idiots! Where are you calling from? Lubyanka? What were they thinking? "If you make a fool pray to God, he'll bust his brain!"—Exactly! And they call him a "shepherd"! It's ridiculous to have pity on these bastards! And besides, he's a "Tikhonite," not a "Renovationist"[125] ... (*chortles*). That's right! After the turpentine enema he'll sing a totally different tune, you can be dead sure of that! And if not, if he's stubborn, tell him you'll cut a cross out of his chest and feed that meat to your fox terrier. By the way, how is that dog? Still limping? Poor boy! Well, bye! Say hello to your wife for me. (*Hangs up the receiver*).

VARVARA (*clenching her teeth, in a nervous trance*): Spawn of Cain! No, wait, more like "convict scum!" The cat will have its fill of the mouse's tears! Don't beg for mercy when it comes, gentlemen Communists. The Russian people suffer patiently, but when their hour of revenge comes the whole world will shake from their wrath. You just wait—they will repay you a hundredfold for the millions of people you've martyred, killed, tortured, humiliated, and who took their own lives in despair! Don't make any pleas then that you're just the peaceful administrator of justice, the guardian of culture! You have showed exactly what "culture" means to the Communist party, that the Party's happy to prosecute free thinkers, how seriously the Party took its slogans of "abolish the death penalty," "abolish war" and "abolish worker exploitation" and all the rest of your promises! You have set the best example of *how* to deal with your enemies! And believe me: Your lesson in mercilessness will not go unheeded by us, when the hour of reckoning comes for your unheard-of atrocities! Beware then, spawn of Cain! Every last one of you will be exterminated, do you hear? Every last bastard one of you!

YAGODA (*in a joyous, satisfied tone*): Well, finally, the true voice of Russian emigration, which has learned nothing during these 20 years and is still living off illusions! Here they are, I was expecting them, the evil thoughts of the incorrigible Russian abroad! It's a familiar tune, it's so familiar that it plays on repeat in the ears of our GPU officers! ... Now I have no doubts about your sincerity, my dear, and I thank you from the bottom of my heart for your frank confession! I was not surprised, I'll say it again! We have known for a long time about the utter nonsense which you Russian refugees feed on abroad. We even prepared a template for this kind of confession of hostility towards Soviet power. Here (*taking a form from the desk and shows it to Varvara*), would you like to sign it later? If you had said something other than that, I would have had doubts about your sincerity. But I need you to be sincere again now in a completely different way. (*He sits down at the table and invites Varvara to take the seat across from him*). Please, take a seat! Tell me! You know your sister better: Is she reliable, can I trust her like I trust myself? This is in an important question for me, right now, because I am surrounded by treachery and betrayal.

VARVARA (*sitting down, exhausted, in front of him and stretching out her hands*): First of all take these … shackles off me!

YAGODA (*gallantly*): Forgive me, I completely forgot! (*Hurries to unfasten her handcuffs while looking into her eyes*): Do you already feel … have you noticed an effect? Are you calmer now?

VARVARA (*throwing the cuffs off*): You might have remembered this sooner.

YAGODA (*smiling*): Errm, no, sorry: With the state you were in, precautionary measures were not at all superfluous.

VARVARA: What a coward!

YAGODA: Just for your own protection! … (*Pushes a form in front of her*): Here, sign this please!

VARVARA (*signing the form almost automatically*): You were asking about Zinaida? (*Returns the form to Yagoda*).

YAGODA (*placing the form in his side pocket*): Yes. Can I rest assured that she and I are of one mind?

VARVARA: She is so under your influence that … It seems to me that she sees everything through your eyes.

YAGODA (*interrupting*): Is she incapable of betraying me? What do you think?

VARVARA: "Betray"? Why should she?

YAGODA: Well, let's say out of jealousy.

VARVARA: And who would be the object of her jealousy? … Are you cheating on her?

YAGODA: "Who"? Well, let us suppose you, for example.

VARVARA (*with a chuckle*): But … we don't have anything in common.

YAGODA: But what if we got to know each other more intimately …? (*Varvara shrugs indignantly*). How would Zinaida react?

VARVARA (*angrily*): Well, how can a decent woman accept such vulgar behavior?

YAGODA: Does she love me that much?

VARVARA: I don't know if she loves you! I know that she cares for you for the sake of her son, whom she really does love more than anything else in the world.

YAGODA: ... And for that she is looking for *support* from me? Is that it? And if that is the case, then there can be no doubt that for the sake of her son, and in order not to lose me as a "resource," she will put up with my infatuation with you, *without protest*.

VARVARA: "Infatuation," yes, but nothing more.

YAGODA (*smiling*): Let's not put the cart before the horse. (*He takes a bracelet encrusted with precious stones out of a box from a table drawer.*)

VARVARA: Oh you wish, you haven't got a chance! I do not understand how you can pursue a woman who despises you like I do!

YAGODA (*laughs lasciviously*): That's what drives me crazy. Don't you know that the more our enemies hate us, the stronger our desire to subdue them becomes? (*He offers the precious bracelet to Varvara*). Would you like a memento of ... your shackles, as you called them?

VARVARA: Oh, if *this* is how you plan to "win" me over, you are sadly mistaken! (*She turns away from him*).

YAGODA (*putting the bracelet away*): Well, I will give it to Zinaida then, see if she refuses it!

VARVARA (*taking a bottle of smelling salts from her purse*): What was that potion you injected me with? (*Smells salt*). It made me feel drunk or ... like I had gas poisoning. Did I babble a lot of unnecessary things to you?

YAGODA (*gallantly*): No, no, nothing "unnecessary"! On the contrary, just what I needed.

VARVARA (*sincerely*): I'm sorry if I offended you, but ... I have quite the temper!

YAGODA (*getting up*): You don't have to apologize! And besides ... Is it possible to be angry with you? You are such a charming woman.

VARVARA (*getting up*): Thank you for the compliment! ... You don't need me anymore?

YAGODA: No, no! You may do as you wish ... (*Looks at his watch*). You'll still be on time to breakfast. I will have my car take you.

VARVARA: You are very kind, thank you! (*She offers her hand to him*).

YAGODA (*kisses her hand*): Goodbye! Give my regards to Zina and tell her that the misunderstanding with customs will be taken care of ... And as for the rest ... (*Puts a finger to his lips*). Hush-hush! Agreed?

VARVARA (*almost coquettishly*): And if I were to tell her everything?

YAGODA (*taking the form signed by Varvara out of his pocket and waving it demonstratively*): Then I shall remember the confession you signed and you won't ever see your sister, or Paris, or your husband, ever again.

VARVARA (*pulling on her gloves, trying to make a joke*): I see that you are quite a *dangerous* Don Juan! Very important to keep this in mind ... (*The both laugh in the most genteel way possible*).

YAGODA: Please, do! I would be flattered!

VARVARA (*continuing to laugh*): There's nothing else left to do ... (*He kisses her hand again and accompanies her to the door*).

YAGODA (*as soon as Varvara has left, he goes to the telephone and picks up the receiver*): Popova's apartment! ... (*Pause*): Is that you, Zina? Hello! Your sister has just left ... I will take care of the misunderstanding with customs regarding her books! But ... I'm only doing this for your sake, as

Varvara Avdeevna flaunts her freethinking much too much. It shouldn't be done! You need to convince her that this is not the right time for it, and that if I were not your friend, she would wind up in the Lubyanka ... By the way, a quick "lyrical digression": You gave me permission to flirt with your little sister, but she is foolishly afraid of becoming a "homewrecker" to you and me ... as if you were a bourgeois and didn't consider jealousy to be a bourgeois prejudice! Tell her, my dear, that "the devil is not as frightful as they paint him," and that it is better to be friends with people like me than to disregard their "advances" ... What? I can't hear what you're saying! "Brothel-keeper"? What does "brothel-keeping" have to do with anything? And who is saying anything about "prostitution"? I am just asking you to explain to her how you see these things, to assuage her conscience. That's all ... (*Pause*). Well, that's silly of you ... So you don't love me after all, and you don't care about what I want? ... (*Pause*). Why are you crying? I will never leave you! And you know that perfectly well, we are connected through our child, and I love him no less than I love you! ... So what are we talking about then? ... I know I have my faults, I know that perfectly well on my own. That is why I am asking for your understanding ... (*Pause*). Fine! We'll talk about it later ... Hugs and kisses! I will give you the bracelet I promised on the day of our munchkin's Octobering. Will you be happy with that? ... Everyone will be green with envy! But don't forget ... about your little sister ... That's it! Don't let her do anything foolish. I've already got my hands full without her ... Well, bye! See you soon! (*He hangs up the receiver, and immediately there is a knock at the door*). Come in!

BULANOV (*poking his head through the half-opened door*): Dr. Levin needs to go to the Kremlin in a hurry—comrade Kaganovich has bad "blood pressure," so ...

YAGODA: I am not detaining him.

BULANOV: Yes, sir! (*Turns around*): Here he is himself! (*Letting Dr. Levin into the laboratory and disappearing, closing the door behind him*).

YAGODA (*to Dr. Levin*): Well, what do you think? Have you figured anything out regarding Yezhov? Do you agree with my directive? There is no more time for hesitation. It's all or nothing!

DR. LEVIN (*squeezing the words out of himself*): I ... agree, but ... on one condition: You must take this murder on your own conscience! ... (*His hands shake as he removes his glasses and wipes the lenses with his handkerchief*).

YAGODA (*amused*): What? "Conscience"?! ... (*Searches his pockets*): And where may I find this "conscience," if I may ask? ... You're an anatomist, a physiologist and a scholar ... When you performed autopsies on corpses, where did you see this "conscience, can you please tell me? ... Aha! Nothing to say?! ... So let's not talk about something that nobody has seen and that, if it exists, only exists in the imagination!

Curtain

Fourth Scene

At the apartment of Zinaida Popova on the day of the child's "Octobering" (the same location as in the first scene).

To the right of the middle door, right next to the wall, there is a table covered in "ceremonial" red cloth bearing the Soviet emblem embroidered in gold. On the wall, above the table, hangs a portrait of Stalin.

Sitting at the table is Bulanov, all dressed up in the "chairman's" seat, with Bukharin on his right and Zinaida Popova on his left. The latter is holding the baby, wrapped in a crimson satin dressing gown and resting on a pillow sewn with rows of magnificent lace. The remaining places at the table are occupied by representatives of the RCP[126] and the Komsomol.[127]

The invited guests (among whom can be seen prominent military officers, Yagoda's co-workers, and artists, co-workers of Zinaida Popova) are seated opposite the "presiding" table and, in part, to the side by the middle door. Some of them are holding large bouquets of flowers, banners with Soviet slogans, and gifts for the person responsible for the "red christening".

The seats closest to the stage lights, and simultaneously to the "presiding" table, are occupied by Yagoda, Rykov, Radek and, next to the latter, Varvara, to whom Radek provides abrupt and rushed explanations of the rite as it takes place.

As the curtain comes up, everyone on stage is standing and singing the last refrain of the "Internationale" to the bravura accompaniment of one of the artists at the piano, after which everyone again takes their seat in the densely packed room.

BULANOV (*unrolling a scroll of paper, addresses those assembled in the usual tone of a professional Soviet orator*): Commencing the meeting of the Presidium of the General Assembly of the collective of the RCP and Komsomol of our Academic Theater, with the participation of the delegates from the heads of the NKVD and the NKGB,[128] I declare that today's Octobering has been organized at the initiative of Zinaida Avdeevna Popova, mother to the subject of today's celebration, and Nikolai Ivanovich Bukharin! (*Hesitant applause*). I consider it appropriate to point out that the petition for this Octobering was made to the Collective by Zinaida Avdeevna, a candidate to our RCP, for her one-year-old male child, the only son of this mother and widow. I therefore propose to recognize the initiative of our esteemed candidate, who has thus facilitated an antireligious civil act! (*All attendees applaud cordially, and Zinaida bows and cheerfully nods her head in gratitude*). I give the floor to this esteemed mother, from whom we look forward to hearing the name which she would like to bestow upon her son.

ZINAIDA (*stands up, gives her child a kiss and speaks in the slightly elevated tone of an actress*): Many wonderful names occurred to me when I began thinking which one of them to pick for my son! Just think: he will carry this name his whole life, and if he excels in his professional field, he will leave a memory of this name for many years! (*Emotionally*): I have devoted all my strength and abilities, all my effort and love to this little man and, naturally, I want him to bear the most radiant, sonorous and remarkable name of our great era. No one would dispute that the most glorious among them is the name borne by our brilliant "Father of Nations"!
Your hand, Stalin, did lead us to fight,
Your thought, Stalin, won our victory bright,

Your eyes, Stalin, surpass the eagle's sight,
With you, our country blooms without blight![129]

In an act of maternal pride, my wish is to give the name of the heir to Lenin, the name Joseph, under whose leadership "our country has blossomed," to my only son. (*The loud applause of the attendees drowns out Zinaida's words. She gives her son a somewhat affected kiss and raises him high, as if showing him off for the assembly*).

BULANOV (*stands up and turns to the representatives of the RCP and the Komsomol, handing the ceremonial paper to them for their signatures*): If there are no objections from the members of the collective of the RCP and the Komsomol, I would ask them to confirm, in accordance with the "Octobering" ceremony, the bestowal of the name of Joseph to the son of comrade Zinaida Popova, candidate to our RCP! (*The members of the collective, including Bukharin, sign the document one by one*). The floor goes to the representative of the Young Pioneers![130] (*An attractive boy about ten years old approaches the "presidium," carrying in one hand a little red flag with the symbol of the Pioneer movement, and, in his other hand, the very same variety of bright-red Pioneer tie that he is also wearing around his neck*).

REPRESENTATIVE OF THE YOUNG PIONEERS (*slightly nervous, pronouncing his speech like a lesson learned by rote*): My comrade pioneers from the ballet studio of the Academic Theater welcome this newborn from the bottom of their hearts and welcome him into our revolutionary ranks! As a token of our comradely regard, today we present him with a uniform tie. I hope that the youngest of the pioneers will wear it with honor, as do his older comrades! (*He presents the red tie to Zinaida, who offers her hand to him in thanks and then returns to her place*).

LAB ASSISTANT (*extravagantly dressed and with coiffed hair, blushing with excitement and even in a sweat, he comes to the table holding a book as a gift*): My unit of the RLYCL[131] authorized me to solemnly declare here our decision to accept patronage over this young citizen, Joseph, and take responsibility for his cultural, political and military upbringing. In token of our pledge, our Komsomol collective presents its young comrade with a copy of the *ABC of Communism*[132] by Nikolai Ivanovich Bukharin, which has taught tens of millions of Soviet citizens how to think correctly about the political system of the USSR! (*Passes the book to Zinaida Popova and, interrupting the applause which was just starting, raises his voice*): I take this opportunity to once again congratulate the author of the ABC on being an authoritative teacher of Marxism, Leninism and Stalinism! (*Stormy applause. Many rise and it becomes a standing ovation to Bukharin. The latter is forced to stand up and bow, with a faint smile*).

BULANOV (*handing the certificate to Zinaida, which by this time has been signed by all the members of the presidium*): The name Joseph has been accepted by the presidium as a maximally significant name, and from now on, for life, it will be borne by the hero of today's festivities. Let us congratulate this citizen of the USSR on his accession to our ranks and wish him success in his service with the young pioneers as well as with the Komsomol, so that he can then become a steadfast fighter for the idea of international revolution and a worthy member of the RCP![133] (*This official portion of the "Octobering" ends in warm and stormy applause. A pianist launches vigorously into the march from "Vesëlye rebiata,"[134] during which the members of the presidium leave their places and, amidst the general hubbub, offer their congratulations to Zinaida Popova. She gives Bukharin a tender kiss, and he then takes the "October Baby" and tends to him until Nanny Zakharovna comes over to them, dressed in an excellent taffeta dress, and takes the baby in her arms. The members of the presidium are followed by the guests, some of whom surround the child and nanny, and others surround Zinaida with their congratulations and gifts. Yagoda, slightly heavy with wine, takes the precious bracelet from a case in his pocket and seizing the moment, presents it to Zinaida. She, indescribably delighted by the generous gift, wraps her arms around Yagoda and, presses against him, kissing him several times, to the general delight of the onlookers. At the same time, the servants, under Varvara's direction, begin serving champagne, sweets and fruit. Some guests empty their glasses immediately, others make their way to Zinaida to clink glasses with her and drink to the health of her heir.)*

ZINAIDA (*seeing Varvara nearby, she calls to her, trying to make herself heard over the joyous hubbub*): Varya, come here! Come, come! Look at this wonderful bracelet that Genrikh gave me! (*Raises her hand with the bracelet on it*). I don't deserve it! It's a museum piece!

YAGODA (*pronouncing his words with "tipsy" boastfulness*): The work of a Florentine craftsman from the 17th century. From the collection of the Ryabushinskys![135]

VARVARA (*to her sister, have recognized the bracelet, without any particular enthusiasm*): Congratulations, my dear! ... Ah! So that's the bracelet he gave you!

ZINAIDA: I really do not deserve it!

BUKHARIN (*to her*): Don't be modest! As an artist and, above all, as a mother, you deserve gifts like that!

ZAKHAROVNA (*emptying her glass of champagne*): That's right, Nikolai Ivanovich! Zinaida Avdeevna has not only sacrificed her life, but you could say, she's given up all of herself for her child. One time the child soiled itself, and another woman would have called the nanny to clean it up, but she did it herself!

ZINAIDA (*kissing the baby in the nanny's arms*): Well, that's natural! What could be sweeter than the feeling of motherhood.

YAGODA: I bow to it and raise my glass in praise of the parents who sacrifice themselves for their offspring!... (*He clinks glasses with Zinaida and drinks down his champagne, to the broken cries of "Hurrah!" from onlookers.*)

BULANOV (*who in the meanwhile has gone into the dining room, together with the pianist and several of the invited artists, returns to the drawingroom and cheerfully "sets things in order," no longer as the "chairman of the presidium" but as the host of the "Octobering"*): Comrades! We are now commencing the artistic program, in which some of our dear lady's colleagues will participate. Your absolute attention and silence are requested. I will take on the role of master of ceremonies—thank God the program is short and I won't have time to bore you! (*Laughter and applause. Little by little, everyone takes their seat amid jokes, merry exclamations and subsiding hubbub*).

BULANOV: The first act in our program will be a reading of Demian Bedny's poem "Us and Them,"[136] i.e., the Communists and the fascists. (*Again there is applause and voices shouting "Yes! Please!"*).

LAB ASSISTANT (*reciting with amateurish emotion*):
Our motherland's path is clear, heroically great,
Unknowably beautiful is its face!
Its mighty genius whirlwind captured near and far, taken all.
Stalin made the joy of life for us, and embodied it in law!
Fascism lives in feverish toil:
Its order is a turmoil,

Labor sweats behind barbed wire,
And "leisure" is in penal servitude.
The legacy of culture burns in bonfires,
And youth's fate is to grow obtuse,
While old age's one cure for grief is death.

But the rebellious Red Front grows,
The fascist nightmare will end:
The proletarian's all-smiting blow
Will bring defeat to him!
(*The audience explodes in applause.*)

BULANOV (*straining his voice to be heard amid the commotion*):
Next up on the program is our favorite singer: The order-
bearer Grigoriev the Second[137] will perform the latest hit,
the song that everyone wants to hear. Can you guess which
one? (*Voices from the audience: "Song of the Motherland!"*[138])
That's right! "Song of the Motherland" …

GRIGORIEV THE SECOND (*taking his place in front of the audience*): I ask all my friends to join in at the end of the cho-
rus … Can I count on you, comrades? (*Voices: "You can! You
can! We give you our word!"*)

BULANOV (*calling everyone to order*): And so, your attention
please! (*Claps his hands and signals to the pianist, who
immediately begins playing the lead-in to the "Song of the
Motherland" with ostentatious energy*).

GRIGORIEV THE SECOND (*sings*):
Wide is my Motherland,
With her many forests, fields, and rivers!
I know of no such other country
Where a man can breathe so free!

CHOIR OF GUESTS (*enthusiastically*):
I know of no such other country
Where a man can breathe so free!

GRIGORIEV THE SECOND:
　　From Moscow to the borders,
　　From southern peaks to northern seas
　　Man goes as master
　　Of his boundless Motherland.

　　Life is everywhere, free and wide,
　　And, like the brimming Volga, flows!
　　The youth are precious to us always,
　　The old are honored everywhere one goes!

　　Wide is my Motherland,
　　With her many forests, fields, and rivers!
　　I know of no such other country
　　Where a man can breathe so free!
CHOIR:
　　I know of no such other country, etc.
GRIGORIEV THE SECOND:
　　A spring wind blows over my land.
　　Every day, living is a greater joy,
　　And on this Earth there's not a one
　　That can outdo us in laughter or in love.

　　But we shall furrow our brows sternly
　　If ever the enemy try to break us,
　　We love our Motherland like a bride,
　　We guard it like a gentle mother.

　　Wide is my Motherland, etc.
　　(*During the last refrain, Zinaida takes the child from the nanny and approaches Bulanov, whispering something in his ear.*)

BULANOV (*at the end of the song and the applause which followed it*): The mistress of the house asks that our dear guests honor the nursery of the little Octobrist with their presence, where we will be playing games, doing dancing rounds and serving tea and sweets. (*Everyone applauds in an outburst of gratitude and, crowding at the door to the dining room, exits through it to the right while murmuring happily, following Zinaida and the Nanny to the nursery. Only Bukharin, Rykov, Yagoda and Radek remain on stage. Yagoda, clearly heavy with wine, sits down to the side and hovers at the edge of sleep.*)

RYKOV (*to the others*): Come on, let's go, or God knows what they will think!

RADEK (*to him*): Wait! Bukharin's got news that concerns us all.

RYKOV: What exactly?

BUKHARIN (*taking a note from his pocket*): A notice for tomorrow's paper! From the prosecutor's office. (*Reads*): "… regarding the statements … made at the trial by some of the accused that Bukharin and Rykov were involved in their criminal activities. The investigation did not find any legal evidentiary basis for holding Bukharin and Rykov legally responsible, as a result of which this case has been closed to any further investigation".[139]

RYKOV: I thought so! Hands can't reach! Daring Joe was afraid to disgrace himself before Europe.

RADEK (*chuckling*): That's Stalin trying to torture me with fear. And I'll say to you, like Lev Tolstoy about Leonid Andreev's stories: "He frightens me, but I'm not afraid".[140] Honestly—I'm not afraid!

BUKHARIN (*pacing around the room and nervously stroking his beard*): Well, no, brother, when you think about all these fake trials and their staging, even looking in from the outside I become afraid, not only for myself, but for our entire homeland! Because if it perishes because of Stalin's policies, we will naturally also perish!

RYKOV: Why yes, another such policy is inconceivable! (*In the distance, to the right, is heard a joyful burst of laughter*). Let's go, comrades, they're waiting for us! (*He heads towards the nursery*).

RADEK (*ignoring Rykov*): It's like a joke: In the 20th year of Soviet power it turns out that everything, everything, from the factory cell to army command is full of traitors and spies. At least that's the conclusion suggested by the court trials, which Stalin is trying to use to strengthen his position. But who will believe it? And could one think of anything more absurd? (*Again a peal of joyful laughter is heard from the guests in the nursery, as well as the sound of the harmonica, to which someone is dancing while others clap in time with their hands.*)

BUKHARIN (*continuously walks nervously around the room, while Rykov stands in an expectant pose, leaning against the middle doorframe*): Indeed! If the charges made by Stalin at these trials correspond to the truth, then the question is, who are all these former representatives of our enormous country? Is it really possible to conceive that one sixth of the world could be ruled by absolute bandits and hardened criminals? If Stalin, by making accusations against all of us, intends to slander us, then one has to ask who is guiding the "greatest state" and with whom do Europe and America have to deal?

RADEK (*in tune with Bukharin*): To put it simply: Who is ruling over Soviet citizens, if yesterday's almighty "minister" turns out to be a "crook," another is a "foreign agent," and a third is a vicious counterrevolutionary who deserves to be in the penal colony!

BUKHARIN: It's inconceivable! How could almost all the founders of Bolshevism become traitors to their party, its precepts, and the entire cause for which they risked their lives, starved in prison and lived as paupers in exile? (*From left to right through the dining room and into the nursery, bottles of wine and all kinds of sweets and fruit are carried in*).

YAGODA (*as if he's waking up in response to all of his comrades' passionate remarks, starts reciting with the gloomy irony of a drunken man*):

O people, people! Sheep, sheep!

I'll teach you all to heed the whip,

I'll make you think whatever I wish,

I'll make you do whatever I need.

O masses, masses! Cattle! Clay!

A wild horde of rams!

There are no parties, say what you may,

There's only the crowd and the men who lead,

Leading the crowd by command ...

BUKHARIN: Where is that from? I seem to know it from somewhere ...

YAGODA: From Bezymensky's play, *The Shot*.[141]

BUKHARIN: Why did you think of it?

YAGODA: Because it depicts Stalin himself, disguised as the party man Prishlyopov.

BUKHARIN: Stalin?

YAGODA: You didn't know? It's all in the past now—we barely managed to hush the whole thing up.

RADEK: What thing?

YAGODA: Oh boy! Weren't you the very first one to point out to Stalin that Bezymensky had written a scathing satire on him?

RADEK (*slightly embarrassed*): I was only joking. Don't you understand jokes?

YAGODA: I know what jokes are ... But *The Shot* didn't just take a shot at Stalin, it "hit the bullseye"—there can't be the slightest doubt about it. That same Prishlyopov says:

I will select from all the ranks

A pack of perfect fools

And very clever scoundrels.

Who'll confidently and without ado

Take good folks for a swindle

As grist for their evil mill.

RYKOV: It really did hit the bullseye. Not a hair's width off the mark.

YAGODA (*with bitter bravado*): And now this "pack of perfect fools" wants to take me out of the NKVD ... eh? What do you think? (*Takes a letter with an "official stamp" out of his pocket*).

BUKHARIN: What are you raving about? Go sleep it off!

YAGODA: But first, read what the Politburo has to offer me. (*Passes the letter to Bukharin; Bukharin, Rykov and Radek all fix their eyes on it.*) They are nominating me for Post Narkom ... eh? How do you like that? To the People's Commissariat of the Post Office! Can you believe the insolence of these "perfect fools"?! Fortunately this "pack" doesn't have a clue about the documents I have in my hands against Stalin! Otherwise they would have taken me out a long time ago, like Kirov, in Leningrad ... And these papers are with a person that—even if Stalin were to arrest me tomorrow—would go present the evidence against him to the right people.

BUKHARIN (*worried*): Well, there you have it! A nice little twist prepared for us by the Politburo! (*Gives the letter back to Yagoda*).

YAGODA: You mean Yezhov?

RYKOV: He means Stalin himself, of course!

RADEK: A "pack of fools" indeed!

RYKOV (*patting Yagoda on the shoulder*): And I was looking at you and wondered: Today you were darker than a rain-cloud ... Looked as though you'd "gone over the edge"! (*Flicks his collar*).

YAGODA (*putting the letter away*): Of course, I won't let anyone see that I slipped on the "shit in the grass". But I swear that I will not let little Joe get away with this. And I'll deal with the "pack of fools" in no time flat! They can be dead sure of that! We know how to handle them ... (*Just before the last words, a choral song is heard from the nursery, imitating children's voices and singing "Once upon a time, grandma had a little gray goat". All four conspirators fall silent, absorbed in their own thoughts. Yagoda, hearing the third verse of "The Little Goat," hurries to add his commentary*): And then we will do the singing (*sings in sync with the choir*):

What's left of Stalin

Are just horns and hooves.

What's left of Cain

Are just horns and hooves.

That's right, that's right,

Just horns and hooves ... etc.[142]

BUKHARIN (*to Yagoda*): From your mouth to God's ears! But for now, we must be very careful: The "maneuvering" has begun, and it's to the death. The "pack of fools" has shown their cards early, and served us very well! (*The servants walk into the dining room from right to left, carrying the dirty dishes, plates with scraps of desserts etc. Varvara follows after the servants, giving directions as she goes. Seeing Bukharin and comrades, she flies into the living room and reprimands them playfully.*)

VARVARA: What is it, comrades? Are you boycotting our games celebrating the new "October tot"? Don't you want to "consecrate" the nursery with your presence? Go, quickly! Or Zina will be very offended!

RADEK (*gallantly*): Ce que femme veut, Dieu le veut! Let's go, comrades, without delay!

BUKHARIN (*to Rykov, with the smile of a gallows-bird*): Come, Alexei Ivanovich! We will enjoy ourselves, "in defiance of the wind and rain". (*Radek, Bukharin and Rykov leave through the dining room, to the right. Yagoda stays behind, blocking Varvara's path*).

YAGODA (*softly, almost "purring"*): May I have a word?

VARVARA (*coldly and brightly*): At your service!

YAGODA (*drunk with wine and lust*): I ... I love you!

VARVARA (*annoyed*): Here you go again!

YAGODA: Again. And I won't give up until..

VARVARA (*interrupting*): I already gave you my answer!

YAGODA (*with irony*): Which was what? Love?

VARVARA: You know my answer! Let's go now, or we will upset Zina. (*Tries to leave, but he stops her, grabbing her by the hand*).

YAGODA: A lot has changed since we last saw each other ...

VARVARA: But not my feelings for you!

YAGODA: You said that you would not lower yourself to be with a "Chekist". But what about the Post Narkom?

VARVARA (*freeing her hand*): What is a Post Narkom?

YAGODA: Well, in France they would call it "Minister of Postal Affairs".

VARVARA (*knitting her brow*): And why should I care?

YAGODA: What do you mean "why"? I gave up my position in the GPU for you, and you don't care? I have sacrificed my entire career for you.

VARVARA (*mockingly*): As if I believe that!

YAGODA: So read it with your own eyes! (*He takes out the letter which he just showed to his comrades and hands it to her. She reads it reluctantly as explosions of laughter, shrill squeals and stamping feet are heard from the nursery: Apparently the guests are enjoying the "active games". After a pause*): Well then? Do you believe I love you now?

VARVARA: Whether I believe it or not makes no difference!

YAGODA: How do you mean? If I'm no longer a "Chekist" to whom you cannot "lower" yourself, then ... (*Embraces her, drawing her towards him*).

VARVARA: Let me go ... you're drunk!

YAGODA: Drunk from my love for you!

VARVARA: Oh, creep!

YAGODA: Just tell me "yes" or "no!": Do you appreciate my sacrifice or not?

VARVARA (*pushing Yagoda away, she breaks free of his embrace*): Leave me alone, you make me sick!

YAGODA (*having nearly fallen over from Varvara's kick, speaks in an angry tone*): Oh, so this is how you're going to speak to me?! ... Beware, sweetheart! I am still in power and I can show you what a risky thing it is to speak such words to me!

VARVARA: Are you trying to scare me again?! ... We're not in the GPU here, this is a private home, thank God!

YAGODA: Wherever we are, I will not allow you to mock me. And not only you, but even Stalin himself won't get away with that! Do you hear me?

ZINAIDA (*appearing in the dining room at the last words, and immediately, having understood what's going on, enters the living room*): Genrikh! Why, my dear, are you keeping everyone waiting? The guests are about to leave, and you haven't paid any attention to them. Do them the honor, at last, or God knows what they will think!

YAGODA (*clicking his heels, smiling drunkenly and winking at Zinaida*): Yes ma'am! Your wish is my command! (*He turns around in military fashion and leaves for the nursery through the dining room*).

ZINAIDA (*to her sister*): What were you arguing about?

VARVARA: We weren't "arguing" about anything, he is simply drunk and pestering me, as if I were some "hussy"!

ZINAIDA: What do you mean, "pestering"? You can't be such a ... prude! We aren't in a monastery, my dear! And besides, Genrikh is so spoiled with women ...

VARVARA: I do not care about that in the slightest.

ZINAIDA (*the bracelet given to her by Yagoda having come undone*): Fasten my bracelet, please. (*Varvara fiddles with the bracelet*). You're wrong ... Well, what does it cost you to give him a minute of joy, when he has done so much good for us!

VARVARA: "Us"? And where do I enter into this?

ZINAIDA: Who went to the trouble of getting you some concessions from customs? Who covered up the business with your illegal books? Who gave me money to help you study in Paris? ... You must show at least a little gratitude.

VARVARA (*pointing to the bracelet*): A hook fell off here. (*Trying to fix the clasp*). I don't understand what you're getting at. I can't be unfaithful to my husband in order to please your lover and generally ... have no shame at all!

ZINAIDA: What shame? What are you talking about, sweetie? Are sexual peccadillos really so disgraceful?

VARVARA (*unable to withstand the weight of her emotions*): Yes! The shame of using *something* that I already rejected indignantly!

ZINAIDA (*raising her eyebrows*): *What* did you reject?

VARVARA: This bracelet! (*Giving it back to her sister*). Here, take it! You only got it because I refused to take it! Do you understand?

ZINAIDA (*putting on the bracelet*): You're joking?

VARVARA: Not at all! Your Genrikh invited me to the GPU and when he saw that I wouldn't give in to him, he tried to buy me off with this bracelet! But he picked the wrong woman!

ZINAIDA (*turning pale*): That's slander!

VARVARA: I swear that it's not! ... And not only are you defending this bastard and not protecting your own ego, but you are also pushing me into his arms ... And for what? To make your life better? Or is it also for the sake of your son? Haven't you sacrificed enough for him? Do you want to sacrifice me for him too? Look out! Today's little "October tot" is starting to look like Moloch, a Moloch who demands more and more monstrous sacrifices. Be careful that this "idol" doesn't turn out to be a vampire who sucks up every last drop of your blood. You've perverted everything, including motherly love. Everything, everything! And if your love for me, as your sister, consists of sharing me with your lover for the sake of your son, then ... God forgive you, my dear, I'm no longer your sister if that's the case, and let's quickly forget about each other's existence!

ZINAIDA (*beside herself with shock*): What is this nonsense you're talking? Are you delirious?

VARVARA: You don't have to believe it, I won't make you!

ZINAIDA: But why didn't you tell me about his behavior *before*?

VARVARA: Because before I was afraid of him, as the head of the GPU.

ZINAIDA (*sarcastically*): And then you stopped? ... (*The telephone rings*).

VARVARA: And then I stopped! Because he's been fired and appointed to another position.

ZINAIDA (*cannot believe her ears*): "Fired" ... Are you crazy? Where did you hear that?

VARVARA: He told me himself and ... showed me a letter to prove it, where he was offered the position of Postmaster General.

ZINAIDA (*with a mocking laugh*): "Postmaster" ...? Maybe even just postman? (*Goes to the telephone*).

VARVARA: Make fun of me all you want! You are living in such blissful ignorance that ... I feel sorry for you, poor thing! I'm sorry for you, because it will be terrible when you "wake up," when you finally understand how things really are!

ZINAIDA (*speaking into the receiver*): Hello! Hello! ... Who is speaking, I don't understand?

VARVARA (*pacing back and forth, nearly wringing her hands in despair*): And why did I come here? That's what I want to know! Why was I pulled into this "hellish paradise," where you have to be a disgusting animal in order to feel good.

ZINAIDA (*into the receiver*): Radek ...? Radek should come down? ... Alright! I'll tell him that they are picking him up.

BULANOV (*appearing on the threshold to the dining room; behind him are several guests; everyone is very drunk*): Zinaida Avdeevna! Why did you leave us? It's all a mess without you. (*There's chatter among the guests: "It's late ... It's time to go home!," "What time is it?," "I have to get up early tomorrow," etc*).

ZINAIDA (*composing herself, like an experienced actress*): Just one moment, just a moment, comrade Bulanov! ... Just ask comrade Radek to come here! They've come for him. (*To the others, after Bulanov runs back into the nursery*). It's still early, comrades! You'll still have time to sit around at home! It's such a big day for me! (*Seeing Radek with Bukharin, with Bulanov beside them*): Ah, yes, Radek, there he is! ... (*To him*): They are waiting for you downstairs! (*Bulanov whispers something to the pianist and sits him down at the piano*).

RADEK: Who?

ZINAIDA: One of your comrades. They said it's important.

RADEK: Why didn't they say who they were? What is this! (*He goes into the foyer; Bukharin follows him. By this time, everyone has returned from the nursery but the nanny and the child. The guests begin to say goodbye to the lady of the house. Rykov and Yagoda are the last to return from the nursery. They are both completely drunk).*

BULANOV (*shouting, jumping up on a chair*): Comrades! Before we leave this hospitable home, let's sing together, like faithful sons of our fatherland, let's sing "The Song of the Motherland". Agreed?

ALL: Agreed! Agreed! Play "Song of the Motherland"! (*The pianist launches vigorously into the song. Everyone sings in a slightly "drunken" voice*):

Wide is my Motherland,

With her many forests, fields, and rivers!

I know of no such other country

Where a man can breathe so free!

BUKHARIN (*rushing in from the foyer, very agitated*): Comrades! ...Wait! ...They just ... they just arrested Radek.

ZINAIDA: What?

BUKHARIN: Radek has been arrested! ... (*General astonishment. Yagoda puckers up his lips toward Varvara, but, losing his balance, he falls down heavily on a nearby chair, while she runs away from him with a disgusted grimace*).

RYKOV (*in a state of bliss*): Oh forget it! ... Jus... just another misunderstanding! ... It's time we get used to it! ... Everything will soon be cleared up and will be shipshape! ... On with the song and to the end of the ball! ... Hey, comrades, let's go! ... (*The pianist repeats the intro. Everyone sings with exaggerated passion*):

I know of no such other country

Where a man can breathe so free!

Curtain
(Second Intermission)

Fifth Scene

At Gorki in Stalin's residence (the same location as in Scene Two).

Once again, it is late at night. The large fireplace on the right-hand side of the study is burning down to crimson embers—the only source of light when the curtain is raised. This light reveals the outline of Stalin's features relaxing at his desk and smoking a pipe, which lends a fantastical and sinister quality to his silhouette.

The "red" dictator is listening to a radio broadcast, which is being transmitted by a top-of-the-line device (and which can be heard before the curtain rises).

VOICE OF SPEAKER ON THE RADIO: *... And only the malicious enemies* of the Soviet Union would dispute that the proletarian court is the only true people's court in the history of the world ... The verdict of such a court is fearsome. And there can be no doubt that it will be able to apply the necessary force in meting out punishment to the new criminals against the state, among whom the official investigation counts such prominent members of the Communist Party and the Sovnarkom as our ambassador in London, our deputy commissar for foreign affairs, our deputy commissar of heavy industry, the commander of the Moscow military district and several others in our party apparatus. These people, who had been invested with the people's confidence, used their authoritative positions not to strengthen our state, but to sabotage its military industry and thereby facilitate the takeover of our national territory by foreign countries.[143] (*A muffled ringing from the telephone on the desk is heard as the last words are spoken*).

STALIN (*switches on the lamp hanging above the desk, and, holding the telephone receiver to one ear and cupping his other ear with his palm, speaks louder than usual to be heard over the radio*): Nikolai Ivanovich …? You brought her yourself? … Well, very good! (*Laughs*). Bring her straight to me. There is no one here now. Come in, no need to knock! … (*Hangs up the receiver*).

VOICE OF SPEAKER ON THE RADIO: These contemptible criminals have now been caught red-handed and they will answer for their evil deeds to the people much sooner than they thought, in their arrogance. Nemesis,[144] the goddess of vengeance, does not tolerate the kind of protracted proceedings that are allowed to take place in the trials of the bourgeois West. Nemesis has become impatient … *Soon, very soon,* all scores will be settled with both the secret and overt enemies of our long-suffering fatherland … Nemesis is impatient. We can already hear the vigorous pace of her approaching footsteps. And we are reminded of the lines of the Soviet bard, who sang the praise of our proletarian Supreme Court:

At the austere table, the judges take their places,

Time marches on and the peoples wait

For their elected Supreme Court

To state its merciless word.

For the bastards and scum,

The vile ones, selling all that they were,

All that's left for them is a single word:

The precise and pithy word of lead!

But we, comrades, do not lose our heads,

And still have time to judge the men

Who would lead the people to the slaughter,

To the triumph of death and destruction!

Time marches on and on, but trust,
That the years do not go by for naught,
That his death will not be of his choice
And only the court will decide his lot![145]

(*The sound of the "Internationale" is heard in the background as Yezhov enters and greets Stalin. Judging by his energetic movements and the expression on his face, he seems to be in an excellent mood. Stalin waves his hand in the direction of the radio set and Yezhov stops the music*).

STALIN (*without letting go of Yezhov's hand*): Does this mean I can congratulate you?

YEZHOV: You bet!

STALIN: Well, very happy for you!

YEZHOV: And I am also—for you.

STALIN: Thank you ... Indeed: "The prey has walked right into the bag".[146] Why did she wait so long to reveal it?

YEZHOV: She can explain it to you herself, it's a delicate matter ... (*Turning towards the door*): Shall I call our little dove in?

STALIN: Go ahead, go ahead! But tell her I don't have long, as much time as the cat has tears.[147] Because I know women: they start pouring out their hearts and then I will have to give up all my work for the day.

YEZHOV: I already warned her! Don't worry! (*Opens the door and calls out*): Comrade Popova, you may come in ... (*A second passes, and Zinaida enters. Bowing to Stalin, she slows down and stops at the door, as if not daring to approach the 'father of nations'. She is dressed in an elegant mourning outfit, which lends itself particularly well to the pathos-laden expression of her face. Zinaida holds a tightly packed briefcase close to her breast*).

STALIN (*without getting up, he nods to her amiably, and, pointing to the chair in front of the table, speaks with the kindness befitting the 'father of nations'*): Hello, my dear! What a beauty you are! Come closer! I won't bite ... I'm so glad to see you. Sit down, you are my guest!

YEZHOV (*to her, encouragingly*): Come here, comrade Popova! Don't be afraid, as he says! (*She approaches the table timidly*).

STALIN (*admiring her*): Here she is, the 'beauty and pride' of the Russian ballet! Just a sight to behold ... Well, sit down and tell us, why do you take to the stage so rarely? Were you ill, or were you abroad on holiday again? By the way, what's the matter with you and Yagoda? Did he make you jealous, or did he do something to hurt you?

ZINAIDA (*sitting down and adjusting her veil*): Oh, you already know why I am here, don't you?

STALIN (*exchanging glances with Yezhov*): "The world is full of rumors".

ZINAIDA: It is not only about me! My business is private and I would not dare interrupt your work because of it, Iosif Vissarionich ... The matter which I discussed with Nikolai Ivanovich (*points to Yezhov with her eyes*), and now your Grace, is a matter of state, one might say ... A political matter! I concealed this business for some time, but now I simply cannot do so any longer. And I have come not only with an accusation against Genrikh, but also against myself: why didn't I reveal this attempt earlier, an attack in the works against both your precious life, and the very foundations of our Soviet state? Do what you want with me, I do not care now: I was an unwilling accomplice to a man who wanted to ruin and disgrace you.

STALIN (*after a short pause, in a tone of great astonishment*): "Ruin" and "disgrace" me? Oh, my! Why, I must ask, because I concealed his expense account "sins" from the Party? ... was it because of this? Or for the fact that instead of sending him to jail, I gave him a place as People's Commissar of Post and Telegraph? What nonsense! You're confused, my dear, or you're slandering your Don Juan out of spite ... Do you think that if he cheated on you, he's also betrayed me? I know women's temperament! You lot have a very special psychology! You forget, my dear, that Yagoda and I have been friends for ten years, and that more than once he has saved me from both enemy machinations and enemy bullets.

ZINAIDA (*with great composure*): He was only waiting for the right moment to destroy you somehow or other.

STALIN: What "moment"? He could have done this a long time ago as the head of the GPU. And as for "disgrace," well ... *how* could he disgrace me? What did he have, I'd like to know? *What*, tell me?!

ZINAIDA (*with the determination of a person throwing themselves into an abyss*): Here's how! (*She opens the briefcase and throws various documents, letters, photographs, and notebooks on the table*). Here is the evidence against you, which Yagoda piled up day by day for ten years.

STALIN (*puzzled, examining the contents of Zinaida's briefcase in a feverish rush*): What is this? What is this evidence against me?

YEZHOV (*as Stalin is examining the "evidence" presented by Zinaida, Yezhov lowers his voice and says to her quickly and tenderly*): Comrade Popova, now that you have admitted your guilt, you only have to make amends, and as quickly as possible. And to do that, first of all, you must name the accomplices to Yagoda's criminal plans.

ZINAIDA (*shrugging her shoulders*): Oh, with pleasure, if only I knew them! But surely you know how cautious and secretive Genrikh was?

YEZHOV: But not with you, my dear, to whom he entrusted these secret documents. Name at least the ones with whom Yagoda made contacts and whom you saw in his entourage.

ZINAIDA (*with a wry smile*): Um ... The ones to whom Yagoda was close he always ... betrayed or destroyed ...

YEZHOV: But not all of them, surely?

ZINAIDA: With a few exceptions. It is strange to say, but his friends were mainly the people he saw as his enemies.

YEZHOV (*smiling*): To creep into their souls, as it were, and ...

ZINAIDA: ... Show them for what they really were.

YEZHOV (*sighing mockingly*): That is the well-trod path of all traitors.

ZINAIDA: If not for these documents, who would have believed that one of Stalin's own friends would ... (*shivers in disgust*).

YEZHOV (*finishing her sentence*): ... would creep up on him, like a viper? ... (*At this time Stalin, who has been examining the documents brought by Zinaida, tears one of them to pieces and crumples the others, muttering to himself: "Son of a bitch! ... what a bastard! ... to trust a man like that! ... the goddamn bloodhound! ... provocateur! ... and he called himself a 'friend'! ... you double-crossing swine!—so that's what the Tsar's secret police teaches you ... a clean job, that's for sure ... stinking spy! ... and you trusted him, God damn it! ...". After Zinaida's last remark, this torrent of curses turns from quiet to thunderous. Stalin, furious, dumps the inkwell over the documents, grabs the envelope in which the documents were kept, and, gathering all of it in his arms, walks over to the fireplace and throws everything into the fire*).

STALIN (*returning to his place, gasping in indignation*): That lousy bastard! He secretly took photos of me when I was drunk or when I was chasing tail! ... Eh? What a backstabber! ... He had to plan for it ... and he's kept a list of every little "foible" of mine! He hasn't left out a single slip! Even had drafts! Picked out resolutions I rejected and kept my signatures, like an extra blunt object up his sleeve to hit me over the head with! (*To Zinaida*): Why didn't you bring me all this garbage earlier, when he was planning to bury me with it, huh?

ZINAIDA: He only gave it to me recently for safekeeping ... And then, I don't care what you think, I still loved him ... and that's why ...

STALIN: You loved a rat bastard like this? This double-dealer? You know he cheated on you left and right! All of Moscow was talking about it.

ZINAIDA: I didn't love him as a man, but as the father of my only child ... On top of that, he terrorized me over the slightest disagreements. You know what kind of terrible power the head of the GPU has!

STALIN (*sternly*): It has already been two weeks since he was removed from his position. Why did you take so long to expose him?

ZINAIDA (*her voice trembles, and she speaks on the verge of tears*): My child was sick. I was beside myself ... I felt crazy! I forgot about everything else!

STALIN (*after a pause, relenting*): Why are you in mourning, and for whom?

YEZHOV (*with the utmost tact*): Her child died, Iosif Vissarionovich.

STALIN: Ah! Well then, I understand everything! (*Stands up and walks to the back of the room in thought*).

ZINAIDA (*sobbing*): He died, my little one! ... He died, and I devoted my whole life to him! Oh God! Oh God! I did everything for him! I sacrificed so much for my little one ... And it was all for nothing! Everything, everything! ... He died, and everything I sacrificed didn't matter, all my sleepless nights didn't matter, my affair with a disgusting man didn't matter. Like he was mocking my motherly love. For what? What did I do? Why am I being punished like this?! ... (*Weeps bitterly. The telephone rings and brings her to her senses*).

YEZHOV (*picking up the phone*): Hello! ... Yes, yes ... I already gave the corresponding orders ... What? ... No, no! Don't let anyone in afterwards ... Alright! I have no time! (*He hangs up the phone*).

ZINAIDA (*standing up and wiping her eyes*): I'm wasting your precious time ... Forgive me, comrades, for my momentary weakness!

STALIN (*giving her his hand*): I deeply sympathize with you and ... I am grateful to you for revealing the truth ... I give you my thanks, not for myself, but for our country! There are so many factions in our country, so many deviations, aberrations and extremes among our party workers, that ... If I had not held the general line in firm hands, the fascists would have taken us with their bare hands ages ago.

ZINAIDA (*heading toward the exit, bowing low*): The entire land of the Soviets is grateful to you for that!

STALIN (*accompanying her to the door*): If there is anything you need, call me: We will arrange for whatever you need! (*Pointing to Yezhov*).

ZINAIDA: I am deeply grateful. For now, I only have one request: Please remove the obstacles to my sister's departure, if Yagoda had made any! He made her sign some outrageous document.

STALIN: Don't worry: everything will be done in the best way. The only thing I want you to do, for now, is to be quiet as a fish! So no one gets off the hook. You understand? (*Smirks*).

ZINAIDA: I understand, Iosif Vissarionovich!

STALIN: Goodbye, my dear!

ZINAIDA: Goodbye! (*Leaves*).

STALIN (*winking to Yezhov*): Well he certainly has good taste, that little clown: what a beauty he snatched for his harem!

YEZHOV: I don't envy him, Iosif Vissarionovich. A nice girl who betrays you at the first opportunity.

STALIN (*sighs*): Yes, on this point you are right!

YEZHOV: Absolutely right, just as I was when I claimed that Yagoda was working against you! Are you convinced now?

STALIN (*throwing up his hands*): Yes, there's nothing else to say about it! And I thought you were just in a hurry to take his place, and so you were using him to scare me for nothing.

YEZHOV (*shaking his head*): How could you say that, Iosif Vissarionovich, do you really think I could do such a despicable thing?

STALIN (*sitting down at the desk*): Well, why do you say "despicable"?! Everyone wants to get a better deal! No man is his own enemy …

YEZHOV: Forgive me, Iosif Vissarionich!

STALIN (*interrupting him affectionately*): Come on, it's nothing! Now the main thing is to find out *who* was this bastard conspiring with.

YEZHOV (*rubbing his hands, smugly*): It's a piece of cake! We will find that out from Radek, who has become even more communicative under arrest than he was before. We just have to give him a good scare and he'll give us who we need.

STALIN (*perplexed*): Why Radek? How could Radek know who Yagoda was conspiring with?

YEZHOV (*explaining delicately*): Very simply, Iosif Vissarionich: Yagoda only rubbed shoulders with those whom he was planning to betray. Yagoda also rubbed shoulders with Radek, as you know, but he did not betray him: it was Zinoviev and Kamenev who betrayed him.

STALIN (*still not understanding*): Well, so what?

YEZHOV: It means that he must need Radek; but Yagoda only needs those who are in league with him, and since Yagoda plotted against you, Radek must have been in league with him too.

STALIN (*in admiration*): Well, brother, you put Sherlock Holmes to shame!

YEZHOV (*modestly*): It is nothing, Iosif Vissarionich! The obviousness of it cries out to be seen.

STALIN (*clapping his hands*): Well, if that's the case, let's go get him quickly! I will interrogate this Robbik myself. Where did you hide him? In the Butyrka?[148]

YEZHOV: I sent him to the secret IZO.[149]

STALIN: Right!

YEZHOV: He begged to see you himself: he wants to complain, claims he is an innocent victim ... And I knew that after Popova's exposure you may need Robbik, and so I ordered him to be brought here.

STALIN (*rubbing his hands*): Well done! The golden head sees everything in advance!

YEZHOV: Robbik will be here at 9 o'clock.

STALIN (*glancing at his watch*): It is already 9 o'clock.

YEZHOV: That means they will announce his arrival. (*Looking at his chronometer*). Your watch is half a minute fast. (*The telephone rings. Yezhov goes to it*).

STALIN (*applauding*): Right on schedule!

YEZHOV (*smiling smugly*): Precision is the first rule in our business. I am very strict in this! (*Speaking into the telephone*): Hello! (*Pause*). Good! Take him right upstairs. (*Hangs up the phone*).

STALIN (*takes out a revolver from the desk drawer and puts it in front of him*): Leave us alone for now, so he won't be shy with an "outsider" here!

YEZHOV: Yes, sir! Remember just to give him a good scare.

STALIN: Don't worry, that's why I took my gun out, as you see. (*There's a knock at the door. Yezhov goes to answer it and, disappearing behind the door, brings in Radek a second or two later. The latter is slightly gaunt, with unkempt and long wild hair; dressed untidily and evidently in a hurry.*)

RADEK (*bowing, not daring to approach Stalin and speaking with a slight stammer*): Iosif Vissarionich, what is the matter? I came to complain about a misunderstanding.

STALIN (*interrupting, with a sneer*): Ah, my friend, hello! You finally played your way to jail did you, you foolish boy? I warned you not to play with fire. And you wanted to pull the wool over my eyes, you little lowlife?! And make me choke on it to boot?! You were preparing an attempt on my life?! You, a friend, who I bared my soul to! Who I told my plans about important things, who I trusted to supervise the Soviet press!

RADEK (*in a neurasthenic trance, speaking almost incomprehensibly, barely speaking Russian*): I assure you that this is a pure misunderstanding. I give you my word of honor! (*Stalin snorts and waves him away contemptuously*). What, is my word of honor not enough for you? Then I will explain everything to you, so you can see!

STALIN (*interrupting*): You will have to explain later, in court. But for now don't bullshit me and tell me straight, who are your accomplices? Well? Tell me, or you'll be sorry.

RADEK (*with a smile on lifeless lips*): What do you mean, "Who are my accomplices"? You know who the defendants in the new trial are, don't you? (*Reciting names like a tongue twister*): Pyatakov, Muralov, Sokolnikov, Drobnis, Shestov, Boguslavsky, Rataichik and Serebryakov.[150] I named about half of them to the Soviet judiciary ... And if they brought me in, it was only because I pretended to be an accomplice, and that was only to find out *which* of them we should worry about, and which we should not.

STALIN (*taking the revolver and twirling it in his hands like a toy*): You're lying, you son of a bitch! Your correspondence with Sedov[151] and Trotsky has *exposed* you completely.[152]

RADEK: What do you mean, "exposed"?! If I were going to be "exposed," I would have to be "posing" to begin with! That is, I would need to be putting on a masquerade. And if a man is naked, even ten strong men couldn't expose him.

STALIN (*tapping the handle of his revolver on the table*): Just make another joke on me, you lousy instigator! Shoot, before a bullet clears a hole through your skull. Are you trying to be funny with me? Huh? Haven't you annoyed me enough with your jokes? Our whole country is fed up with them: they make us sick!

RADEK: What "jokes"? What have jokes got to do with it? ... Laugh at me or don't laugh at me, but I'm not interested in jokes right now. And really, what a "*Missinverständnis*" [sic!] this is![153] A man gets arrested for nothing, for zilch, and they put him in jail! What a fine thing! What for, I'd like to know? Because I always denounced those who were suspected by the party? Because I exposed "strategizers" like Marszałek[154] Pan Tukhachevsky? And because none of the counterrevolutionaries could chować away[155] from me? Why was I imprisoned, proszę pana?[156]

YEZHOV (*dryly*): Because you did not denounce *yourself* first of all! And you should have started with that!

RADEK: "Myself"? That's a good one! And what was I guilty of, that I should denounce myself? That's easy to say!

YEZHOV: You're guilty of criminal concealment, for starters! And, second, of being party to a conspiracy against the party!

RADEK: But I explained already that it was done *on purpose*, to find out *which* of the conspirators were real, and which were only fooling around, to impress others. And if I did not manage to report on time, then, excuse me, but we are not at the horse-racing track, where we need to rush along at a breakneck speed!

STALIN (*placing the revolver on the table with a clatter*): Enough talk! Either you immediately give up the accomplices of the new plot, or I will not let you even live to see the trial, you despicable traitor!

RADEK (*trembling, with a guilty smile*): But whom do you want me to betray? Give me a name, and I will confirm czy to tak, czy nie![157]

YEZHOV: Bukharin!

STALIN: Rykov!

RADEK (*looking at them like a cornered animal*): Bukharin and Rykov? That's a good one! You know from the newspapers that the prosecutor has no legal data to prosecute them.

YEZHOV (*sharply*): This was published at my request, so they would put their guard down and allow us to see who they are connected with ... (*A pause: it is as silent as the grave*).

STALIN (*to Radek, in a hollow voice, breathing heavily*): Give your answer on Rykov and Bukharin immediately!

RADEK (*wriggling like a worm in a flame*): What should I answer you, if you are better informed than me. (*Chuckling*): It is *I* who should ask you, not *you* who should ask me!

STALIN (*hissing*): Why didn't you inform on them?

RADEK (*in a choked voice*): Because I didn't know ...! Yes. I didn't know!

STALIN (*savagely*): You didn't know with whom you were plotting against the Party and planning an attempt on my life?

RADEK (*half-dead from fear*): I swear I didn't know that it was so serious! I thought, as usual, that it was just "talk".

STALIN (*picking up his revolver*): Don't lie, you son of a bitch, or I won't be responsible for what I do next!

RADEK (*hysterically*): But I swear! I swear by the most sacred thing that exists for me: the Communist Party, for which

I risked my life! ... What more do you want from me? Why are you tormenting me? Do you want me to swear it on my knees? Or you won't believe me otherwise? (*Falling to his knees*): Here, I swear on my knees, by God, that what I am saying is true! (*He begins to whimper pitifully, takes out his handkerchief and blows his nose tearfully. Stalin exchanges a glance with Yezhov and nods his head toward the door*).

YEZHOV (*looking at his watch*): I have an urgent matter, so if you don't mind ...

STALIN (*to him*): Go on, my dear, I will deal with this bastard on my own.

YEZHOV (*with a wry grin*): Enjoy yourselves! (*Leaves*).

STALIN (*after him, not without irony*): Thank you kindly!

RADEK (*crawling on his knees in front of Stalin, almost shrieking*): Oi, what are you doing to me?! And for what, I want to know?! If I've wronged you, then I was still your friend and good adviser! Or is all that forgotten already?! Have you forgotten that *I* was the one who denounced Gamarnik and Kork? That *I* was the one who tracked down Uborevich in connection with Tukhachevsky? Forgotten *what* I wrote in *Izvestia* against the Zinoviev gang? That I demanded that the "mad dogs" be publicly executed?!! Have you forgotten everything? Even the fact that I was the *first* to prompt Ludendorff[158] to allow us to travel here in a sealed train car?! Then read Fritz Platten[159] and what he writes in *Die Reise Lenins durch Deutschland im plombirten* [sic] *Wagen*![160] You can't deny all a man's merits and judge him a crook! I was the secretary of the Zimmerwald Conference and secretary of the Third International!

STALIN (*harshly*): Regardless of your position, you were always a bastard by nature and a scoundrel who should have been shot a long time ago!

RADEK (*persuasively and ingratiatingly*): Well, maybe I am a bastard! But why should I be shot if I can still be useful to the Party? Didn't Lenin teach that "some bastards are valuable precisely because they are bastards,"[161] because a bastard can do things that an honest fool just can't do! Wasn't it also Lenin who taught us how to infiltrate the trade unions, permitting us to go along with "all sorts of tricks, stratagems, illegal methods, lies by omission, and concealing the truth".[162] It's even printed in the complete collection of his works.

STALIN (*putting the revolver on the table*): Well, that's it! I will spare your lousy life, but on one condition: hand over *everyone* who was in league with Bukharin, Rykov, and you. Do you hear, *all of them*, even those who you are afraid to give away!

RADEK (*rising from his knees*): But, if you'll allow me, Iosif Vissarionovich! ...

STALIN (*interrupting*): I won't allow anything! Give them up now, or there will be consequences. (*Picks up the revolver again*).

RADEK (*clears his throat and says, looking away*): Krestinsky![163]

STALIN: The ambassador in Berlin?

RADEK: That's right!

STALIN: Who else?

RADEK: Rakovsky![164]

STALIN: The ambassador in Paris?

RADEK: That's right!

STALIN: Who else?

RADEK (*hesitating confusedly, struggling*): Hmm ... There are so many of them.

STALIN: That's irrelevant!

RADEK (*almost singing, smiling in embarrassment*): Chernov, Rozengoltz, Bezsonov, Grin'ko, Sharangovich, Khodzhaev,

Ikramov, Maksimov-Dikovsky, Kriuchkov, Dr. Levin, Pletnev, Kazakov[165]... that's all of them!

STALIN (*stomping his foot*): No it isn't! ... I know who else you were plotting with, against the party and against me. And if you don't give me his name right this minute, don't expect any mercy for yourself, Radek!

RADEK (*hesitating*): Oh my God, did I really forget someone?, hmm ... Who could I have forgotten? God help me remember ... (*pause*). Ah, yes, I remember! ...

STALIN: Well?

RADEK: (*lowering his head, speaking faintly*): Genrikh Yagoda!

STALIN (*satisfied*): There we are! (*Opens the desk drawer and places the revolver in there with a thud*). Lucky for you! ... You may go! ... (*Radek lowers his head even lower, as if bowing, and walks out of the room taking small steps*).

Curtain

Sixth Scene

The office of the People's Commissar of Internal Affairs, N.I. Yezhov, newly decorated and furnished. This is the same office in the building of the NKVD that is described in detail in the Judicial Report on the case of the anti-Soviet "Right-Trotskyite bloc" regarding the poisoning of the air in an attempt to assassinate Yezhov. (See the 1938 issue of Iuridicheskii Izdatel'stvo, *Moscow, pp. 492–494 ff.).*[166]

There are three doors at the back of the stage: the door on the right leads to the inner premises of the GPU; on the left, to the foyer and the "waiting room"; and, in the middle, to a corridor that connects with the secret premises of the GPU. All three doors are curtained with heavy drapes; when they are thrown open, GPU guards are invariably seen behind them, guarding the office and the adjoining rooms.

There is very little furniture in the room, which is decorated in a cold, uncomfortable "official" style. On the right, close to the stage lights, is the massive desk of the People's Commissar; behind it is a large armchair, and on the sides of the table are two smaller ones.

Behind the table, on the wall, are monumental framed photographic portraits of Stalin, Lenin and Felix Dzerzhinsky.

The curtain rises to show Yezhov seated in the presiding seat; to his right, at the narrow end of the table (facing the audience) is Prosecutor Vyshinsky, who, in the trial of the anti-Soviet bloc, is also fulfilling the role of investigator; opposite him, with his back to the audience, is his secretary; opposite Yezhov, that is, to the left, sits Bukharin, arms crossed over his chest.

While the court personnel look relatively healthy and neatly dressed, Bukharin is strikingly emaciated, his face thin, with a

*sickly blush, a feverish gleam in his eyes, and moves his arms
and legs in nervous jolts, as if they do not obey him.*

PROSECUTOR VYSHINSKY: ... And I will repeat my question: do
you confirm *this* conversation with Marshal Tukhachevsky,
or do you not?

BUKHARIN: In Hegel's *Logic* he considers the word "this" to
be the most difficult.

PROSECUTOR VYSHINSKY (*to Yezhov*): Comrade President,
I request that you clarify for the defendant Bukharin that
he is here for questioning not as a philosopher, but as a
criminal, and it would be better for him to keep quiet about
Hegelian philosophy, at least out of respect for Hegelian
philosophy ...!

BUKHARIN: Can a criminal not be a philosopher?

PROSECUTOR VYSHINSKY: He can! But not when he resorts
to tricks, trying to confuse the investigation for the sake of
self-defense.[167]

BUKHARIN (*irritated*): There is nothing for me to defend! In
this case, I would be better suited to be the accuser! And if
I am defending something, then it is not my own interests,
but the interests of the entire Communist Party, which Stalin has turned into "voting sheep"!

PROSECUTOR VYSHINSKY (*with a mocking smile, as if to say
"by the way"*): ... and for this you decided to dispose of him
without a shred of remorse?

BUKHARIN: No one can speak of conscience when it comes
to Stalin, especially after he discredited Soviet democracy,
destroyed Party cadres, organized an assault on the Komsomol, and staged trials, which, by the absurd nature of the
charges, have even surpassed medieval witch trials.

PROSECUTOR VYSHINSKY (*chuckling*): Thank you very much! But your plan to arrest him had already taken shape by 1918.

BUKHARIN: Not only to arrest Stalin, but Lenin too. But that was just "talk".

PROSECUTOR VYSHINSKY (*to Yezhov*): I petition for the "left communists,"[168] who Bukharin led in the early years of the Revolution, to be summoned as witnesses.[169]

BUKHARIN: It is a great pity that we abandoned that plan at the time! Then we would not have to argue now about a regime that allows its heroic founders to be condemned! About a government that destroys those who were its leaders and humble toilers! A proletarian republic that has abolished freedom of labor, and where workers are chained to factories like slaves!

PROSECUTOR VYSHINSKY (*ironically*): It is certainly commendable that you confess your criminal intention, but far from commendable that they should set it into motion. You know that it smacks of Article 58 of the Penal Code,[170] which is subject to *the death penalty*. And frankly speaking, you have nothing to be angry about, because you *yourself*, in your "Communist Program," convincingly proved that the proletarian state, like any other, is an *organization of violence*. Am I quoting you correctly?[171]

YEZHOV: "Anyone who is afraid of being subjected to violence by the proletarian state,"[172] writes Bukharin, "is not a revolutionary at all."

PROSECUTOR VYSHINSKY (*to Bukharin*): Not even ten days after you yourself, in the Politburo, threatened to use capital punishment against those who deviated from the line you saw as correct.[173]

YEZHOV: No need to protest now! You argued for the death penalty yourself.

PROSECUTOR VYSHINSKY: So the question is whether you want to die without repenting for your errors to the proletariat, to die, so to speak, "like a dog,"[174] or whether you want to repent before that, and thereby render a significant service to the Communist Party.

YEZHOV (*to Bukharin*): You always taught from your pulpits and in your books that our Party is the bearer of the true doctrine that is immutable for a true Marxist, that its leaders can make mistakes, but the Party itself remains unshakeable in its main principles?

BUKHARIN (*through clenched teeth*): I will do the party a great service if I can expose Stalin as the "usurper" he is, rather than sign my name to the guilt that you attribute to me, just to compromise our righteous cause!

PROSECUTOR VYSHINSKY (*coldly*): Your choice!

BUKHARIN: I am not afraid of being shot, and you will not frighten me with death. But before I fall under the Chekists' bullets, believe me, I will make good use of my defendant's bench as a tribune of honor!

PROSECUTOR VYSHINSKY (*sneering*): Don't think that you will get away with it unpunished! (*Exchanges glances with Yezhov*).

BUKHARIN (*defiantly*): *What* should I be afraid of, if I am going to die no matter what?

YEZHOV (*clearing his throat*): Didn't Yagoda tell you that proven counterrevolutionaries do not all die ... in the same way?

BUKHARIN (*after a short pause of perplexity*): How do you mean "not in the same way"?

YEZHOV: Well ... In order for a criminal to be sentenced to a normal death ... he has to earn it! (*Writes something on a notepad and hands the note to the secretary*).

BUKHARIN: How?

Prosecutor Vyshinsky (*slipping a sheet of paper covered in small script to Bukharin*): Here I have formulated what kind of repentance we expect from you at the court. Read it attentively and give me the paper with your signature ... (*The secretary exits to the right with Yezhov's note*).

Bukharin (*having glanced at the prosecutor's sheet, he slams his hand on it in indignation*): What is this nonsense? What kind of insinuations are you giving me to sign? I ... I do not know what basis you had for turning me into a "spy". I only know that nothing in the world will make sign my name to these vile deeds, of which I am not guilty in either word or thought. (*The secretary returns to his place*).

Prosecutor Vyshinsky: So you flatly refuse to acknowledge that you have been serving the fascists for all these years ...? And do this despite the facts testified to by your friends?[175] (*He writes something on a scrap of paper and hands it to Yezhov*).

Bukharin (*angrily*): Who are these "friends"? It's just as difficult to believe that you, a *prosecutor*, are serving in the same trial as an *investigator*. This is unheard of in the history of the courts!

Yezhov (*to Bukharin, sternly*): Well, well! Don't forget where you are!

Prosecutor Vyshinsky (*to Yezhov, with a knowing smile*): Then I make an immediate request for a cross-examination between the accused and ... another witness.

Yezhov (*giving Vyshinsky's note to the secretary*): Please fulfill the Prosecutor's request! (*Secretary exits to the right*).

Prosecutor Vyshinsky (*to Bukharin*): Your obstinance is pointless, since your friend Rykov has already signed his name to the same kind of document.

Bukharin (*stunned*): Rykov? Alexey Ivanovich, former Chairman of the Council of People's Commissars?

PROSECUTOR VYSHINSKY: Well, of course! Why are you so surprised? (*He shows Bukharin one of the documents in his folder*). Take a look for yourself, if you like! (*Bukharin, beside himself with agitation, examines the sheet, while Vyshinsky rubs his hands, exchanging glances with Yezhov*).

BUKHARIN (*his goatee quivering*): Although I already have a poor opinion of our Soviet court, I confess that I would never in my life have believed that it would go so far as to accuse a man using *deliberately* falsified facts. I am completely disgusted and nauseous!

PROSECUTOR VYSHINSKY: It's no use trying to wrap yourself in the lily-white robes of the conceited bourgeoisie! If necessary, the Bolshevik Party has the right to demand from its members any kind of statement, self-denunciation, and even self-incrimination for whatever the Party dictates for political expediency! (*Yezhov nods his head, repeatedly confirming the prosecutor's words*). As a Communist Party official, you should know that a Bolshevik has no need to talk mellifluously about his *own* honor when the Central Committee of the Party demands that a member of the Party "tarnish" their reputation in a public trial! (*At the last words, the secretary appears to the right, accompanied by Radek. The latter is impeccably dressed, shaved, with a fresh haircut, and has the appearance of a person satisfied with his fate. The secretary shows him to a chair near Prosecutor Vyshinsky and returns to his seat*).

RADEK (*bowing to Yezhov and Vyshinsky*):[176] It's my honor to bow to you, my dear esteemed citizens! I will be sincerely happy to help the justice department sort out our devious affairs! (*As he takes a seat in response to Yezhov's gesture of invitation, he turns to Bukharin with a cheeky look*): Hello, comrade ... (*Bukharin frowns*). I mean "comrade in misfortune". What's the matter? I have a feeling that you are refusing to admit something which is completely superfluous to deny! We have been caught red-handed, and we only have to confess *honestly* that we organized this espionage on Trotsky's orders, so he has nowhere to hide!

PROSECUTOR VYSHINSKY (*to him, in a quiet tone*): Rykov has told us in quite some detail how the party of antagonists to Stalin's policies was formed in your conspiratorial group, and how you transitioned to committing terrorist acts. Now I would like to know how the defendant Bukharin not only participated in the espionage activities of the "Trotskyite bloc," but was directly involved in Marshal Tukhachevsky's military conspiracy.

RADEK (*with hurried servility*): It is very easy to find out! Just ask citizen Bukharin czy[177] he was liaising with Polish espionage, czy he wasn't.

BUKHARIN (*looking at the ceiling*): I will not stoop to dignify such questions with an answer!

PROSECUTOR VYSHINSKY (*to him*): You have no reason to make a stern face, defendant Bukharin! You must admit to what there is, whether you want to or not. And here's what there is: you had a group of accomplices in Belarus, headed by Chervyakov, Goloded and Sharangovich ...[178]

RADEK: Absolutely right!

PROSECUTOR VYSHINSKY: ... According to your directive, these persons contacted Polish Intelligence and the Polish General Staff.

RADEK: Absolutely right!

PROSECUTOR VYSHINSKY: Therefore, *who* organized the spy ring that these individuals were involved in?

RADEK: Rykov and Bukharin!

PROSECUTOR VYSHINSKY: So, can we consider you a spy, or not?

BUKHARIN (*to Vyshinsky*): Consider me whatever you want! I do not intend to nod along with you in this false report![179]

RADEK: Why "false"? Why are you so distrustful of my words? You were always so attentive to my remarks ...!

BUKHARIN: And I have no intention of talking to you, you vile traitor!

RADEK (*with a superior smile*): "vile traitor" ...? That's a good one! Why am I a "vile traitor," please explain! Because I am in favor of disclosing the truth to the judicial authorities? Or because my memory is better than yours when it comes to espionage? (*To Yezhov and Vyshinsky*): Why am I a "despicable traitor," I'd like to know?

BUKHARIN: Because you know as well as I do that I have never been a spy, and could never be one by my nature, although I did believe that in Belarus and Ukraine life would have been better under the rule of fascist intellectuals than under the rule of a monster like Stalin.[180]

RADEK (*to Yezhov and Vyshinsky, with the passionate tone of an informer*): Do you hear how this madman thinks? It's just one step from this to opening a front to the enemy, and to thereby destroying all Soviet power.

PROSECUTOR VYSHINSKY (*to Bukharin*): What, in particular, was the role you took upon yourself among all those spies, subversives and simple murderers who terrorized our government?

BUKHARIN (*in a "professor-like" tone*): I was engaged in the *theoretical problems* of general leadership and the *ideological aspect*, which of course did not exclude my awareness of the practical side of things.

PROSECUTOR VYSHINSKY (*with undisguised mockery for Bukharin, addresses Yezhov, looking for his support*): Please, assess the role of this gentleman who is allegedly involved not in directing all kinds of crimes, but in the "theoretical problems" of those crimes, not in organizing those monstrous crimes, but in the "ideological side" of this dark business! As you have heard, Bukharin, caught red-handed, calls in Hegel as his witness, rushes into the wilderness of linguistics, philology and rhetoric, murmurs some scholarly words, just to cover up the evidence any way he can.[181] I have never heard of another example in which a spy and a murderer would use philosophy like sand to throw in the eyes of his victim before smashing his head in!

RADEK (*to Bukharin, not without pathos, and with an obscene swagger*): Shame on you, Bukharin! It is shameful to be duplicitous before our comrade investigator, who is tirelessly working to untangle the knotted muddle of your state crimes. You must be *honest* in your repentance when you are caught red-handed. You must confess your guilt honestly and indicate, without exception, your closest accomplices in the case. *Honesty* is the sacred duty of every Bolshevik towards the Party and its judicial authorities! Take an example from me, citizen Bukharin! Have the courage, at least, to confess your counterrevolutionary deeds and to confess your state crimes.

YEZHOV (*glancing at his watch*): Thank you, witness Radek! (*to Vyshinsky*): Comrade Prosecutor has no more questions for the witness?

PROSECUTOR VYSHINSKY: Thank you. I am fully satisfied with the cross-examination.

YEZHOV (*to Radek*): In that case, you are free to go. (*To the secretary*): Please escort the witness out!! (*The secretary stands up to carry out the order*).

RADEK: (*with disgust*): Shame on you, citizen Bukharin! (*Bows low to Yezhov. Proudly raising his head like a man who has fulfilled his duty, he departs to the right, accompanied by his secretary.*)

PROSECUTOR VYSHINSKY (*to Bukharin, twirling the paper which he gave the defendant to sign*): So you flatly refuse to sign that you worked as a *spy* for the fascists, and that this was why you traveled abroad so often?

BUKHARIN: I do not change my words every ten minutes!

PROSECUTOR VYSHINSKY: That is a pity, because your sincere repentance could have earned you a lighter sentence.

BUKHARIN (*laughing*): It would have served me right to believe you! I bet Zinoviev and Kamenev were also probably promised to have their lives spared, but were shot treacherously anyways.

PROSECUTOR VYSHINSKY: You would be wrong! Soviet power honors its word, and, especially, any witnesses who might be useful to it more than once.

YEZHOV (*to Bukharin*): Didn't your friend Yagoda tell you about his idea of "*execution in the hereafter*"?

BUKHARIN: "Execution in the hereafter"?

YEZHOV: Well, yes! The so-called "second death"? (*To the secretary, who has returned to the office*): Did you prepare the condemned I told you about?

SECRETARY: Yes, sir! They are ready for you.

YEZHOV: Bring them here! (*The secretary goes to the middle door*).

PROSECUTOR VYSHINSKY (*to Bukharin*): Now you will see your mistake …

YEZHOV (*gets up and, interrupting Vyshinsky, addresses him*): Do you want to take a break?

PROSECUTOR VYSHINSKY (*stands up*): I have nothing against it.

YEZHOV: Let's go to the cafeteria for a minute and wet our gullets.

PROSECUTOR VYSHINSKY: Much obliged! (*Both of them head to the right door, just as Zinoviev and Kamenev, accompanied by the secretary, emerge from the middle door. Behind the doors we can clearly see the prison guards on duty*).

YEZHOV (*turning to the secretary as he exits*): Break time! You can take a load off. Are the guards on duty?

SECRETARY: Yes, sir!

YEZHOV: Come along! (*All three exit to the right. Bukharin, unable to believe his eyes, walks up to Zinoviev and Kamenev and looks at them as if they had just returned from the dead. In fact, they look like ghosts, with their sullen looks, gaunt, grayish faces and frayed, faded clothes*).

BUKHARIN (*after a pause*): I never thought I would see you alive …! What does it mean?

ZINOVIEV (*in a stifled voice, looking around*): It means there is a hell …

BUKHARIN: "Hell"? How do you mean?

KAMENEV: We mean it literally!

ZINOVIEV: They said it was just something the priests invented but hell really exists, and it is unimaginable!

BUKHARIN: What nonsense! Explain what you're talking about.

KAMENEV: Well … It is very simple: In the newspapers they announce to the relatives that such and such criminals have been shot, but they are simply listed as dead so they can be treated however their captors please: beat them for nothing, feed them all kinds of rotten food, and torture them to death.

ZINOVIEV (*in a hurry to have his say*): I was lashed so hard with a cane a day or two ago that I still cannot sit down … This is something unheard of!

KAMENEV (*to Zinoviev*): And all because you bicker with the guards … Take me for example: I am like a lamb. If they tell me to write memoirs, I write memoirs; if they tell me to clean the outhouse, I clean the outhouse; if they tell me to eat a piece of soap when they've had too much to drink, I eat it without a whimper ... That's why I became the favorite death row inmate.

ZINOVIEV (*to him*): You have no self-respect! It's easy for you. But not everyone is like you!

KAMENEV: Self-respect? Why the hell would a dead man need self-respect? What kind of self-respect can dead men have? Officially, we don't even exist, so our self-respect also no longer exists.

ZINOVIEV: That's just an empty paradox! I can't believe that when you ruled Moscow you were considered Russia's premier libertine.

KAMENEV: You should forget about it, because the more you remind prisoners of their former greatness, the stronger their desire to strike you in the face. "Former Chairman of the Comintern"? Well, knock him down so he won't get a big head!

ZINOVIEV (*to Bukharin*): My best advice: agree to any self-denunciation! Sign off on any crime! Agree to play the most humiliating role in the trial! As long as they *actually* shoot you, and not just on paper! Because it is worse than death! A thousand times worse!

BUKHARIN (*bewildered*): Didn't you scourge yourself enough in court to deserve a normal death?

ZINOVIEV (*bitterly ironic*): We confessed to 60%, and Stalin wanted us to confess to the whole 100%.

KAMENEV: There's just been a misunderstanding, and we haven't lost hope ...

BUKHARIN (*shocked*): Of committing suicide?

KAMENEV: Of requesting permission for it.

ZINOVIEV: Otherwise, it is inconceivable! (*Pointing at the door*): There are "watchmen"[182] on the lookout everywhere.

KAMENEV: If they see you being listless, you can either eat nothing or eat scraps. Every hell has its own underworld.

ZINOVIEV: They are also under strict observation.

KAMENEV: Remember Trotsky's words: "In the basements of the Lubyanka, suicide is an inaccessible luxury".

BUKHARIN (*walking diagonally across the room*): So what does it all mean? The trial between the authorities and the defendants doesn't take place in court, but behind the scenes; in Party committees, and not in the organs of the judicial investigation; in the Commissariat of Internal Affairs, and not in the Judiciary!

KAMENEV: Is this really news to you?

ZINOVIEV: Did you come from outer space, comrade?

BUKHARIN (*suddenly stops, remembering something*): I am not your comrade, after the way you betrayed me! And I still don't understand how in hell you could do something so vile!

ZINOVIEV: Is it really our fault that we were drugged by the GPU with some bilge that weakens people's will, and causes a fit of honesty?[183]

BUKHARIN (*skeptically*): What "bilge"? Stop making things up!

KAMENEV (*grimly ironic*): Yagoda's pride and joy.

BUKHARIN: Wasn't he also the one who invented "execution in the hereafter"?

ZINOVIEV: Well, who else could invent something like that?

KAMENEV (*feverishly*): Is it true that *he* also fell in Stalin's trap?

BUKHARIN: You mean Yezhov's?

ZINOVIEV: Right, Yezhov's! There's a rumor floating around here.

BUKHARIN: It's true! Yagoda is under arrest and is being tried together with us.

KAMENEV (*almost jumping from Schadenfreude*): Oh so he'll finally find out what "execution in the hereafter" is like!

ZINOVIEV: I'll make him pay for everything, that God-damned fraud!

KAMENEV (*still triumphant*): A place in hell for the devil! He paved his own way here. I swear the tables have turned. (*Yezhov returns from the right, accompanied by Vyshinsky and the secretary; all three, evidently, have had a few drops of "refreshing" liquid*).

YEZHOV (*to Bukharin, chuckling*): Well, how are our bullet-riddled friends doing? Have you seen how hale and hearty they are?

PROSECUTOR VYSHINSKY (*to Bukharin*): Did they bring you around?

YEZHOV: As you see, it is up to you to choose how you will die. Think about it and give us your answer tomorrow ... (*As he sits down at the table, to the secretary*): Release the defendant and send the condemned inmates away! (*The secretary takes Bukharin to the right, and Zinoviev and Kamenev to the middle door*).

PROSECUTOR VYSHINSKY (*taking his seat, glancing at the file*): Today we finish Yagoda's interrogation, and that of his assistant Bulanov.

YEZHOV (*playfully, snapping his fingers*): And one more individual.

PROSECUTOR VYSHINSKY (*looking at the file again*): Ah yes of course! Two cross-examinations at once.

YEZHOV (*seeing the secretary returning*): Bring in Yagoda and Bulanov.

SECRETARY: Yes, sir! (*Exits to the right*).

YEZHOV (*to Vyshinsky*): In your opening statement you need to emphasize as strongly as possible that all these Trotsky-ites, Zinovievites and Bukharinites are nothing but *capitulators*. That, concealing themselves with revolutionary phrases, they were seeking to re-establish capitalism in

Russia. And when did they want to do this? At the very moment our country began to experience the joys of the communist system, the system that turned poor, backward Russia into the richest and most powerful proletarian state.

PROSECUTOR VYSHINSKY (*writing down Yezhov's words as if "taking dictation"*): The gospel truth! And you said it perfectly, Nikolai Ivanovich ... (*At this moment the secretary brings in Yagoda and Bulanov. Both defendants look a little "stunned," although they try to hold themselves together*).

YEZHOV (*to Yagoda and Bulanov*): Sit down! (*Points to the seats in front of him and addresses Vyshinsky, who is finishing his notes*): You wanted to continue the interrogation of the defendants ...

PROSECUTOR VYSHINSKY: Right away! (*Putting the papers in front of him in order*).

SECRETARY (*to Yezhov*): May I ask Yagoda a question?

YEZHOV: Be my guest!

SECRETARY (*to Yagoda, looking through his papers*): When were you *baptized*?

YAGODA (*not comprehending*): "Baptized"?

SECRETARY: Yes. What year did you join the Tsar's service?

YAGODA: At the beginning of the war.

SECRETARY: But not before? (*Takes notes*).

YAGODA: No. Before the war there was no sense in taking refuge in the Tsar's secret police. But when they began a draft for the front lines ... Well, then it was different![184] (*Chuckles*).

SECRETARY (*takes notes, smiles*): I see!

PROSECUTOR VYSHINSKY (*to Yagoda*): Returning to the attempt on Comrade Yezhov's life, our Commissar of Internal Affairs (*bows slightly toward Yezhov*), I would like to clarify the details of the poisoning of his office. (*Points to the surrounding walls*). What can you add to your testimony?

YAGODA: I did not do this out of personal revenge, but to save myself and the conspirators, whom Yezhov had already begun to destroy. The poisoning of this room (*looks at the walls*) was actually performed not by me, but by Bulanov. (*Points to Bulanov, who is seated nearby*).

PROSECUTOR VYSHINSKY (*to Bulanov*): What can you say about this?

BULANOV: I do not know a damn thing about chemistry or medicine. And yet, on Yagoda's orders, I mixed mercury with acid and ordered him to spray this mixture on carpets, curtains, and tablecloths. (*Points to the table*). We took the sprayer from Yagoda's lavatory[185]... And, I must say, we sprayed everything down thoroughly, so that Nikolai Ivanovich would die here just from inhaling the poison (*bows toward Yezhov*); but clearly I didn't get the chemistry right, so our efforts were a waste of time!

YEZHOV (*laughing*): Ay-ay-ay! How could you let Genrikh Grigorevich down like this? He must have been quite sad about this failure, eh? (*Vyshinsky and his secretary also start laughing*).

BULANOV (*to Yezhov, lowering his gaze*): If I had not failed, it wouldn't be *you* sitting in the chairman's place, but Genrikh Grigorievich.

YEZHOV: And I'd be sitting in his place?

BULANOV: If you had survived. (*General laughter*).

YEZHOV (*to Yagoda*): No, really, Yagoda, why didn't you just sneak up on me and kill me? It would have been much easier!

YAGODA (*chuckling*): Thank you very much! So we could get some witnesses and have to go justify ourselves before Stalin?

BULANOV (*nodding*): And our way was "clean as a whistle" ...

YEZHOV (*finishing Bulanov's sentence*): ... until we discovered everything. (*General laughter*).

YAGODA: Well, who could expect someone to stab me in the back? Lucky for you a bitch like that was so close to me!

YEZHOV (*interrupting*): Quiet! ... What's the use of that kind of abuse now, when there's no point? (*To Vyshinsky*): Do you have any more questions for Bulanov?

PROSECUTOR VYSHINSKY: Yes! I would like to establish whether or not the defendant sent money to Trotsky?

YAGODA (*reacting angrily*): I did not send any money to Trotsky.

PROSECUTOR VYSHINSKY: Really?

BULANOV (*to Yagoda*): I think you forgot, Genrikh Grigoriev-ich! (*To Vyshinsky*): Two years ago, Yagoda warned me that a man would come and that I should give him twenty thousand *dollars*. And when I later reported that this order was carried out, Yagoda told me to continue to give this man subsidies for Trotsky, because he was quite desperate.[186]

PROSECUTOR VYSHINSKY: And what was the name of this intermediary between Yagoda and Trotsky?

BULAN: (*rubbing his forehead*): Hm ... Mirov-Abramov.[187]

YAGODA: I categorically deny that I sent money to Trotsky, and I've never heard of this Mirov-Abramov.

PROSECUTOR VYSHINSKY: Perfect! We will now check this thoroughly. (*He writes a note and hands it to Yezhov, who, smiling, hands it to his secretary, who exits with it to the left*).

YAGODA (*somewhat shaken*): I couldn't have forgotten that ...! However, in my position I had to meet with so many people, that ... Anything is possible, of course ... (*The secretary brings in Zinaida Popova from the waiting room to the left. She is no longer in mourning; she is dressed in the latest Parisian fashions of 1936–1937. Yezhov shakes hands with her and gently sits her down between him and Vyshinsky, facing Yagoda).*

PROSECUTOR VYSHINSKY (*to her, bowing slightly*): We have again called you in to clarify a very important question: when Yagoda, being in the position of Commissar of Internal Affairs, in other words, when he was sworn to protect us from enemies such as Trotsky, did he send money to Trotsky abroad?

ZINAIDA (*thinking*): I can't say exactly, but ... In general, Yagoda often entrusted me with giving money to certain people ...

PROSECUTOR VYSHINSKY: For example ...? To whom ...?

ZINAIDA: Dr. Levin, Pletnev, Kazakov ...

PROSECUTOR VYSHINSKY: And was money ever given in dollars?

ZINAIDA: Yes it was.

PROSECUTOR VYSHINSKY: To whom, for example?

ZINAIDA (*remembering*): Well, for example ... to Mirov-Abramov.

PROSECUTOR VYSHINSKY (*writing this down quickly, with a smile of satisfaction*): To Mirov-Abramov. (*After a pause, to Yezhov*): I have no more questions for the witness. (*To her*): Thank you very much.

YEZHOV (*stands up and offers his hand to Zinaida*): Comrade Popova, you are free to go! (*To the secretary*): Let Bulanov go as well! (*The secretary takes Bulanov to the door on the right, and returns to his place*).

ZINAIDA (*shaking hands with Yezhov*): My sister asked me to thank you for your assistance in her departure. She was deeply moved by your kindness.

YEZHOV: When is she leaving?

ZINAIDA: She already left yesterday on the express train.

YEZHOV: I heard that you are also going to Paris to visit her?

ZINAIDA: Yes, but it will be after the end of the trial.

YEZHOV: But of course!

YAGODA (*standing up, to Yezhov*): Please allow me to pose a question to Ms. Popova.

YEZHOV: Please!

YAGODA (*slightly nervous*): You are taking my child with you, aren't you? I would like to see him before you go.

ZINAIDA (*with intentional cruelty*): Your child is dead ... he died ... You didn't know that? Then know that he's gone! And thank God that the last link between us has been severed with his death! Nurturing your offspring, the offspring of the greatest criminal in the world, lying constantly for you, humiliating myself by conversing with you, and pretending to love you, is too much for me now! (*Suddenly remembering something, she takes a precious bracelet given to her by Yagoda out of her purse and places it on the table*). Even the memory of our baby's "Octobering" has become a burden to me, and I am giving this "souvenir" back to you! (*Yagoda is about to reach for the bracelet, but Yezhov snatches it before him*).

YEZHOV (*examining the bracelet*): Well, well! Where did this bracelet come from ... from the "Historical Museum"?! (*Looking into Yagoda's eyes*): Yet more evidence of your plundering of state property! ... How low you have fallen, my dear! (*To Zinaida, bidding her farewell*): Thank you for that extra touch to characterize my ... predecessor!

ZINAIDA (*giving him her hand*): Goodbye!

YEZHOV: Take care! (*She nods her head to Vyshinsky, and exits to the left*).

PROSECUTOR VYSHINSKY (*to Yagoda*): I do not understand one thing: how could you "serve two masters" for so long: the party, headed by Stalin, and his enemies, headed by Trotsky?

YAGODA: What is there not to understand? Life is a game, and sometimes we have to bet on two horses at once! One will win, and from that one you'll have something to take home ... I was betting on both Stalin and Trotsky at once.

PROSECUTOR VYSHINSKY: Yes, but your political sympathies ...?

YAGODA: What god damned "sympathies"! ... (*Rises and rubs his limbs, stretching slightly*). Neither the Trotskyite program nor Trotsky himself ever aroused the slightest sympathy in me. But as the head of the GPU, I knew perfectly well the hatred that people have for Stalin. So I was waiting to see which "horse" would win in the competition, and I got ready in advance to join the side that would come out on top.

PROSECUTOR VYSHINSKY: Cynical! But ... At least it's honest!

YAGODA: Why should I be shy about anything, when the gig is up and I no longer need a mask!

PROSECUTOR VYSHINSKY: "Mask"? What mask?

YAGODA (*sighing*): I have been wearing a *mask* all my life, pretending to be a Bolshevik, and I never was!

PROSECUTOR VYSHINSKY: So why did you pretend?

YAGODA: Because I could feel it in the air that the Bolsheviks' time would come, and then we would start dividing the wealth of the bourgeoisie! (*Rubbing his hands*). And I'll get my share! ... And I'm not the only one who *played a role*, but almost everyone, starting with Stalin ... Just look at what is happening now on *the stage* of Russia! Everyone in power *uses a pseudonym*, just like in a *play*, wearing *masks*, using secret passages, *pretending* to be loyal subjects of Her Majesty the Party, and groveling to its leaders, who they try to snatch by the leg and throw into the basement of the Lubyanka. It's just one big *comedy*: a comedy of serving the people. A comedy of adoring the leaders! A comedy of the court and making human sacrifices! Even a comedy of the death penalty! A pompous *joke* of a *theatrical show* or a bloody *melodrama*, like the ones that they used to write for the entertainment of the unwashed masses! That's what our life is like now. Some people play the role of the "noble fathers of the people," some play the role of "denouncers and traitors," some play the role of "femme fatale," and some play the role of "executioners"! (*Pointing at himself*). And this entire absurd *performance* is played with a straight face, as if it were a witty "revue"!

PROSECUTOR VYSHINSKY (*with a wry smile*): And at whose expense?

YEZHOV: At the expense of the people, the poor idiots who'll spend their last penny on this "spectacle".

YAGODA (*chuckling*): Well, you might as well ham it up if the people will put up with spectacles like these!

Curtain

Notes

1 "There is no gentle path that leads from the earth to the stars ..."
   (Lucius Annaeus Seneca).

2 As can be seen from the text of the play, Evreinov was still in the
   process of writing the play until at least 1941 (see below).

3 A reference to what are known as the three "Moscow Trials". These
   were show trials held between 1936 and 1938, in which a number
   of party leaders from the early post-revolutionary years were pros-
   ecuted, along with numerous minor functionaries and random individuals. A characteristic element of these judicial "performances,"
   which were intended to have a significant national and international
   impact, was that the defendants were not tried for actual or alleged
   oppositional political views, but for completely fictitious, almost
   absurd charges, including plots to murder Stalin and other prominent figures or acts of sabotage and espionage on behalf of capital-
   ist or fascist powers. The 1st Moscow Trial, officially the "Trial of the
   Trotskyist-Zinovievist Terrorist Center," held August 19–24, 1936,
   was directed against former leading members of the Left and United
   Opposition of 1923–1927 (Zinov'ev, Kamenev). The 2nd Moscow Trial
   (January 23–30, 1937, "Trial of the Anti-Soviet Trotskyist Center")
   also targeted former Left Oppositionists (Radek, Sokol'nikov, Pyatakov). Finally, the 3rd Moscow Trial, conducted as the "Case of the Bloc
   of Rights and Trotskyites" from March 2–13, 1938, persecuted both
   former members of the "Right Opposition" in the party (Bukharin,
   Rykov) and former Trotsky supporters (Krestinsky, Rakovsky), as
   well as the former chief of the secret police, Genrikh Yagoda, and a
   number of doctors and scientists. The supposed fulcrum of all these
   fictitious conspiracies was claimed to be Lev Trotsky, Stalin's most
   prominent opponent within the Communist Party, who was expelled
   from the country in 1929. Almost all of the defendants in the three
   show trials were sentenced to death and shot.

4   The second half of the 1930s was a decidedly inauspicious time to stage a play critical of Stalin in France. Strong pro-Soviet sentiments prevailed during the Popular Front government of 1936–1937 and for some time following; in 1940, a large part of France was occupied by Nazi Germany, which was at that moment allied with Stalin; and, finally, from 1941, the Soviet Union became an ally in the fight against Germany. See the essay by Gleb Albert on pages 29–50.

5   The *Report of Court Proceedings* of the 3ʳᵈ Moscow Trial, published in 13 languages and running 800 pages long in the English edition, is not at all an uncensored transcript of the trial. It is the result of a meticulous but simultaneously brutal editing process in which Stalin participated personally. A comparison with the unpublished original transcript reveals that numerous passages in which the defendants pointed out contradictions and sought to defend themselves were deleted; some statements were completely deleted or rewritten. See Wladislaw Hedeler, "Ezhov's Scenario for the Great Terror and the Falsified Record of the Third Moscow Show Trial," in *Stalin's Terror: High Politics and Mass Repression in the Soviet Union,* ed. by Barry McLoughlin and Kevin McDermott (Basingstoke: Palgrave Macmillan, 2004), 34–55.

6   *Pavel Abramovich Berlin* (1878–1962): Russian journalist. Lived for a time in Zurich and Berlin before the Revolution, returned to St. Petersburg in 1907, finally emigrated to Paris in 1922. Wrote actively in both the liberal and social-democratic émigré press.

7   The Russian artist and stage designer *Ivan Bilibin* (1876–1942), who designed costumes for Evreinov's Ancient Theater, fled Soviet Russia in 1920 and settled in Paris in 1925, but after helping to design the Soviet embassy building in Paris in 1935, he returned to the Soviet Union the following year, where he was able to work as an artist and lecturer. He died during the Siege of Leningrad.

8   The conductor *Mikhail Shteinman* (1889–1949), who left the Soviet Union in the late 1920s and became a central figure in the musical

life of the Russian exile community, returned to Russia in 1937 and was able to continue working as a conductor.

9   The composer *Sergei Prokofiev* (1891–1953) emigrated in 1918, but was already returning regularly to the Soviet Union to perform in the late 1920s and early 1930s. He moved back permanently in 1936. He became one of the most prominent composers of the Stalin era and was awarded six Stalin Prizes.

10   Prokofiev's wife, the Spanish singer *Lina Prokofieva* (1897–1989), born Carolina Codina, came to the Soviet Union with her husband and received Soviet citizenship. The couple separated in 1941, and Prokofieva was arrested in 1948, accused of espionage and sentenced to twenty years in a camp. She was released in 1956 and was not allowed to leave the Soviet Union until 1974. The US journalist *Edmund Stevens* (1910–1992), mentioned in Anna Kashina-Evreinova's footnote, was a Moscow correspondent for *The Christian Science Monitor* and, as became known only after the Soviet archives were opened, an informant for the Soviet secret services. In 1950 he was awarded the Pulitzer Prize for the 44-article series "This is Russia Uncensored," in which he described various facets of life in the Soviet Union.

11   Christian Science is a religious organization founded by the American Mary Baker Eddy in the 19th century. Christian Science practitioners are trained to heal others through prayer.

12   *Viktor Grigorievich Fink* (1888–1973): Soviet writer and translator, stayed in France in 1937 while working for Soviet cultural institutions.

13   Fink graduated from the Sorbonne Law School in 1913 and was in Paris during the outbreak of the First World War. He volunteered for the Foreign Legion and returned to Russia in 1916.

14   A line from a popular song by Vasilii Lebedev-Kumach (lyrics) and Isaak Dunaevskii (music), originally for the film *Tsirk* (*The Circus*) directed by Grigorii Aleksandrov (1936, see below).

15   *Zinov'ev, Grigorii Ievseevich* (born Radomysl'skii, 1883–1936): political writer and activist in Russian Social Democracy, later one of the leading early Soviet politicians. Son of a dairy owner. After the 1903

party split, he became a prominent Bolshevik and one of Lenin's closest comrades-in-arms in exile. After the October Revolution, he was
chairman of the Petrograd Council of People's Commissars and the
Comintern, and a member of the Politburo of the Communist Party
from 1921 to 1926. In the wake of Lenin's serious illness in late 1922,
as part of a "troika" together with Kamenev and Stalin, he became one
of the de facto leaders of the Soviet Union. Having been instrumen-
tal in ousting Trotsky from politics in 1923–1924, he opposed Stalin
himself in 1925 and was one of the leaders of the "United Opposition," which was finally forced out of positions of power by Stalin's
faction in 1927. Expelled from the party in 1927, he was sentenced to
four years of exile to Kazakhstan in 1928. Restored to the party in 1933
after recanting his opposition activities, he was nevertheless arrested
again in 1934 in the aftermath of the assassination of Leningrad party
leader Sergei Kirov, sentenced to death at the 1st Moscow Show Trial
on August 24, 1936, and executed two days later.

16   Comintern: aka the Communist International and Third International. An international association of Communist parties founded
in Moscow in 1919 on the initiative of the Bolsheviks as a counter-
model to the social-democratic Second International. Although the
member parties formally functioned as equal sections of the Comintern, the Soviet party dominated the organization morally, structur-
ally, and, last but not least, financially. Under Stalin, the Comintern
ultimately degenerated into an instrument of Soviet foreign policy
and foreign intelligence. After its leadership, which had remained
international in character, was decimated disproportionately by
the Great Terror, the Comintern was dissolved in 1943 on Stalin's
orders. The Comintern was chaired by Zinoviev until 1926, then by
Bukharin until 1928.

17   Northern Commune (full name: Union of Communes of the Northern
Territory): administrative unit of the Soviet Union that existed from
1918 to 1919. The Northern Commune included the northwestern
provinces of Russia, with Petrograd as its administrative center.

18   *Kamenev, Lev Borisovich* (born Rosenfel'd, 1883–1936): writer and activist in Russian Social Democracy, later one of the leading early Soviet politicians. Son of an engine driver. Prominent Bolshevik after the 1903 party split and close ally of Lenin and Zinoviev in exile. His wife was Ol'ga Kameneva, Lev Trotsky's sister. He briefly served as chairman of the Bolshevik faction in the St. Petersburg Duma in 1914, was arrested and exiled after the outbreak of the war. As a politician he was known for his moderate and conciliatory line, which was regularly held against him by Lenin and others. Nevertheless, after 1917 Kamenev took a prominent political position, including being a member of the Politburo and chairman of the Moscow Soviet. Initially part of the "triumvirate" with Stalin and Zinoviev, he became one of the leaders of the "United Opposition" along with the latter and was ousted in 1927. Restored to the party in 1933, thereafter held several literary-academic posts, including director of the Academy Publishing House in 1933–1934 and director of the Maxim Gorky Institute of World Literature in 1934. Arrested in 1934 in the aftermath of the assassination of Leningrad party leader Sergei Kirov, he was sentenced to ten years in prison in 1935. In 1936 he was sentenced to death in the 1st Moscow Show Trial and executed together with Zinoviev.

19   Council of People's Commissars (*Sovet Narodnykh Komissarov*, SNK): supreme executive body of the Soviet Union; people's commissariats corresponded to ministries. Kamenev was only deputy chairman of the Council of People's Commissars, but in November 1917 he was briefly chairman of the General Central Executive Council (VTsIK) and thus de facto the first head of state of the Soviet Union.

20   Council for Labor and Defense (*Sovet truda i oborony*, STO): government body created in 1920 and dissolved in 1937, focusing on economic and financial coordination under civil war conditions. Kamenev headed the council from 1924 to 1926.

21   *Rykov, Alexei Ivanovich* (1881–1938): activist in Russian Social Democracy, after 1903 one of the leaders of the Bolsheviks. Came from a peasant family. After the October Revolution, he became first

People's Commissar of the Interior, then occupied high party and state posts, including as a member of the Politburo and chairman of the Supreme People's Economic Council (VSNCh). From 1924 to 1930, chairman of the SNK and thus formally head of government of the Soviet Union. Ousted from the highest offices in 1930 as one of the spokesmen of the so-called "Right Opposition," People's Commissar for Posts and Telecommunications from 1931 to 1936. In 1937 he was finally expelled from the CPSU and arrested. He was sentenced to death in the 3rd Moscow Show Trial on March 13, 1938 and executed two days later.

22   *Bukharin, Nikolai Ivanovich* (1888–1938): activist of the revolutionary student movement in Russia, later a leading Bolshevik. Son of a teacher. A member of the party from 1906, he distinguished himself early as a publicist and economic theorist. After the October Revolution, Bukharin held high state and party posts and was one of the party's leading theoreticians. He was an early supporter of the theoretically unsophisticated Stalin, with whom he was on first-name terms, and formulated, among other things, his doctrine of "building socialism in one country." Bukharin was ousted from high politics after 1929 as a spokesman for the so-called "Right Opposition," but nevertheless remained an important journalist, philosopher, scholar and press official. Editor-in-chief of *Pravda*, editor-in-chief of *Izvestia* from 1934 to 1937. Was arrested in February 1937, wrote memoirs and philosophical works in prison. On March 13, 1938, he was sentenced to death in the 3rd Moscow Show Trial and executed.

23   In Russian *Izvestiia TsIKa Soiuza SSR I VTsIKa Ispolkoma Sovetov*: this was the full title of the daily *Izvestiia*, founded in March 1917 as a newsletter of the Petrograd Soviet, which functioned as an official government organ in the following decades and is still published today.

24   Most likely a fictitious person. Neither a Popova nor a Descourcel (see below) is mentioned in the authoritative biographies of Bukharin. See Stephen F. Cohen, *Bukharin and the Bolshevik Revolution:*

A Political Biography, 1888–1938 (New York: Vintage Books, 1975); Wladislaw Hedeler, *Nikolai Bucharin: Stalins tragischer Opponent – Eine politische Biographie* (Berlin: Matthes & Seitz, 2014).

25 Most likely a fictional person. Original spelling: Dekursel'. This was the Russian transcription of, among others, the French playwright Adrien Decourcelle (1821–1892), so the decision was made here to transcribe the surname of the fictional person following this French surname.

26 *Vsesoiuznaia kommunisticheskaia partiia (bol'shevikov)* (All-Union Communist Party [Bolsheviks]). From 1925 to 1952, the official name of the Communist Party of the Soviet Union. Stalin assumed the newly created, initially purely administrative post of general secretary in 1922 and developed it into the most powerful position within the party.

27 *Iagoda, Genrikh Grigor'evich* (1891–1938): Soviet party and intelligence official. Son of a goldsmith. Initially an anarchist, later a Bolshevik activist, and after the October Revolution collaborated in the Cheka, the Soviet secret police, in which he soon assumed leading positions. From 1927 deputy head of the OGPU, from 1934 head of the NKVD (see below). The GULag network of penal camps was established in the Soviet Union under his leadership. In September 1936 Yagoda was removed from his position and, after a brief interlude as People's Commissar for Telecommunications was arrested on March 28, 1937. He was sentenced to death in the 3rd Moscow Show Trial on March 13, 1938, and executed two days later.

28 *OGPU*: also often known as the GPU, short for *Ob''edinennoe gosudarstvennoe politicheskoe upravlenie*, the Joint State Political Directorate. From 1922 to 1934, the name for the Soviet secret police. Successor organization to the Cheka founded by Felix Dzerzhinsky in 1918. In 1934 Genrikh Yagoda became the head of the OGPU. Under Yagoda, the OGPU merged into the People's Commissariat for Internal Affairs (NKVD) later that year.

29   People's Commissariat for Domestic Affairs (*Narodnyi komissariat vnutrennykh del, NKVD*): Ministry of Domestic Affairs of the Soviet Union, led by Genrikh Yagoda between 1934 and 1936, then by Nikolai Ezhov from 1936 to 1940.

30   *Bulanov, Pavel Petrovich* (1895–1938): Soviet secret police functionary. Son of a forester, he joined the Cheka in 1921 and quickly made a career for himself. He had already become responsible for repressions against prominent political opponents of Stalin, including Trotsky, by the end of the 1920s. He was de facto Yagoda's right-hand man, one of the main organizers of the 1st Moscow Show Trial. In March 1937 he was dismissed from the NKVD for economic offenses and arrested. One of the defendants in the 3rd Moscow Show Trial, sentenced to death on August 13, 1938, and executed two days later.

31   *Ezhov, Nikolai Ivanovich* (1895–1940): Soviet intelligence officer, one of the main organizers of the Great Terror. Son of a house painter. Red Army officer, made a party career in the 1920s. From 1934 to 1939, chairman of the Commission for Party Control of the CPSU Central Committee and secretary of the CPSU Central Committee; from September 1936 to April 1938, People's Commissar of the Interior of the USSR, during which time he worked in intense cooperation with Stalin. Arrested on April 10, 1939, he was sentenced to death on February 3, 1940 for alleged preparations for a coup d'état.

32   Commission for Party Control (Russian *Tsentral'naia kontrol'naia komissiia VKP(b)*, TsKK for short; from 1934: *Komissiia partiinogo kontrolia pri TsK VKP(b)*. Disciplinary and control body of the VKP(b). The Party Control Commission supervised the discipline and morale of party members and could decide on party expulsions. Was headed by Ezhov from 1935 to 1939 (de facto until 1938).

33   *Radek, Karl Berngardovich* (born Karol Sobelsohn, 1885–1939): Austro-Hungarian, Polish, and Soviet revolutionary, journalist and politician. Son of a postal clerk, he was a member of both Polish and German Social Democracy and was close collaborator with Lenin in

European exile. Joined the Bolshevik Party in 1917, became one of the most prominent Soviet propagandists and journalists, as well as a Comintern functionary. Initially a central member of the Left Opposition around Trotsky, he was expelled from the party in 1927. After a public confession of repentance in 1930, he again became active as a journalist, an expert on international relations, and an adviser to Stalin. He was arrested in September 1936, sentenced to ten years in prison as a defendant in the 2nd Moscow Trial on January 30, 1937. Murdered in prison on May 19, 1939, allegedly by criminal fellow prisoners. It was only recently proven that his murderer was in reality an NKVD functionary who had been imprisoned for official misconduct and charged with the murder by the highest authority, and who was released a little later as a reward for his deed. The decision to have Radek murdered had been made after he had spoken openly with other prisoners about the trials being staged. See Nikita V. Petrov, *Pervyi predsedatel' KGB Ivan Serov* (Mocow: Materik, 2005), 313–315.

34 Zimmerwald Conference: clandestine gathering of anti-war socialists held in Zimmerwald, near Bern, Switzerland, September 5–8, 1915. Thirty-seven participants from twelve countries attended, including representatives of various strands of the Russian revolutionary movement. Although the conference adopted the Zimmerwald Manifesto condemning the war, a minority around Lenin, Zinoviev and Radek, the so-called "Zimmerwald Left," could not accommodate their clearly more radical demands in the document, namely the transformation of the imperialist war into a revolutionary civil war.

35 *Vyshinskii, Andrei Iakovlevich* [actually: Ianuarievich] (1883–1954): Soviet politician, jurist and diplomat. Born to Polish nobility. Initially a Menshevik and opponent of Lenin, he crossed over to the Bolsheviks in 1920, and after this rose quickly in his political career. From 1931 to 1939 he served as Prosecutor General and prosecutor at all major show trials. From 1940 he continued his career as a diplomat and died of a heart attack in New York in 1954.

149

36   *Levin, Lev Grigor'evich* (1870–1938): Soviet physician, one of the chief
     physicians of the Kremlin Hospital, attending physician to Maxim
     Gorky as well as to Lenin, Yagoda, and many other prominent party
     officials. Arrested in December 1937, he was sentenced to death in the
     3rd Moscow Show Trial on March 13, 1938 and executed two days later.

37   The GPU's toxicological laboratory, about which very little con-
     firmed evidence exists, was established in the early 1920s to develop
     biological and chemical methods of killing. Yagoda is commonly
     credited with a large part in this work. The laboratory continued to
     exist after the Stalin era and probably still exists today.

38   The wedding scarf (Russian: *ubrus*) is a festive headscarf worn by the
     bride in the traditional peasant wedding ritual and kept for life after-
     wards.

39   In the Russian original: *Oktiabriny*, translates roughly as an "Octo-
     ber baptism". Together with the "red funeral," the "October bap-
     tism" was one of the post-revolutionary rituals launched after the
     Civil War to replace church rites. In addition to speeches and gifts,
     the "October baptism" included giving the child a name (as "revolu-
     tionary" as possible). Despite intensive propaganda in the press and
     literature, this ritual never gained widespread acceptance. By the
     1930s, it was hardly practiced at all anymore.

40   This was a popular phrase derived from Lenin's statement on the New
     Economic Policy (NEP) in his speech to the 9th Congress of Soviets
     (December 23–28, 1921). It is open whether Evreinov knew the full
     quote, in which Lenin conceived of the NEP as designed to last for
     a long time, but explicitly not for eternity: "… we shall carry out this
     policy in earnest and for a long time, but, of course, […] not for ever."
     See Vladimir I. Lenin, *Works*, vol. 33 (Moscow: Progress Publishers,
     1966), 160.

41   *Chekist*: term for member of the secret police. ChK, often written out
     in English as it is pronounced in Russian—Cheka—is the abbrevia-
     tion for the Extraordinary All-Russian Commission for Combating
     Counterrevolution, Speculation, and Sabotage (Russian: *Vserossiis-*

kaia chrezvychainaia komissiia po bor'be s kontrrevoliutsiei, spekuli-
atsiei i sabotazhem), the secret police of Soviet Russia established
after the October Revolution on December 20, 1917. Its successor
body was the GPU (see above).

42 A reference to Zinaida Popova's late husband.

43 In the original, *niania*: Russian for "wet nurse" or "nanny".

44 In spoken Russian, the -ovich ending in patronymics is often compressed into a -ych.

45 A reference to the 1st Moscow Show Trial (see above).

46 On August 21, 1936, Radek, already threatened with arrest himself,
published the article "The Trotskyist-Sinovievist Fascist Gang and its
Whip Trotsky," in *Izvestiia*, directed against the defendants in the 1st
Moscow Trial, which was also published in the international com-
munist press, including the *Basler Rundschau* (August 27). It culmi-
nated in a call to "eliminate" the "monsters." See Wladislaw Hedeler,
Chronik der Moskauer Schauprozesse 1936, 1937 und 1938: Planung,
Inszenierung, und Wirkung (Berlin: Akademie Verlag, 2003), 74, 76.

47 Throughout his life, Radek had a reputation for both being fond of
telling political jokes as well as being the author of many such jokes.
He was also explicitly accused of this in the Stalinist press in 1937.
See Aleksandra Archipova and Mikhail Mel'nichenko, *Anekdoty o*
Staline. Teksty, kommentarii, issledovaniia (Moscow: OGI, 2011), 25.

48 *Zinoviev Bloc*: aka the "Trotskyist-Zinovievite Terrorist Center". A fictitious conspiracy said to have been the work of various mostly high-
ranking party and state officials who had also taken positions critical of Stalin's policies in various episodes of early Soviet history. The
individuals grouped under this fiction, established by Stalin and the
secret police, were tried in the 1st Moscow Show Trial in 1936 for the
murder of Leningrad party leader Kirov and for planning other alleged acts of terrorism.

49 The Bolsheviks initially referred to the penal camps they had set up as
"concentration camps" (Russian: *kontsentratsionnyi lager'*, abbreviated to *kontslager'*), in keeping with the international term established

already before World War I. It was not until 1929 that the Politburo decided to rename the camps "labor reform camps" (*ispravitel'no-trudovoi lager'*, abbreviated ITL). See Oleg V. Khlevniuk, *The History of the Gulag: From Collectivization to the Great Terror* (New Haven: Yale University Press, 2004), 32.

50 *White Sea Canal, Russian: Belomorkanal*: 227 km waterway connecting Lake Onega to the White Sea. Built between 1931 and 1933 on Stalin's orders and under Yagoda's direction. Political prisoners were used in its construction; tens of thousands died because of the poor conditions.

51 *Narym (Narymskii krai)*: A region in Siberia whose center is the small town of Narym, which had already been an important place of exile in pre-revolutionary times. Stalin, for example, was himself deported there in 1912. Under Stalin's rule, the area became one of the centers of the GULag system. In the summer of 1933, the so-called "Nazino tragedy" occurred at the village of the same name near Narym, when over 6,100 prisoners were abandoned on a river island without food. More than 2000 of them died of starvation and disease.

Solovki: island archipelago in the White Sea near Arkhangelsk. The first Soviet labor camp was established here in 1921. It was under the control of the GPU and laid the foundation for the later GULag system. It was the primary place of detention for political prisoners in the 1920s, including many non-Bolshevik socialists and later members of the Left Opposition.

52 *Maksim Gor'kii* (real name Alexei Maksimovich Peshkov 1868–1936): Russian and Soviet writer. Author of socially critical prose and plays in the pre-revolutionary period, member of the God-building movement (*bogostroitel'stvo*), close to the Bolsheviks. After the October Revolution, initially skeptical of the new regime, he lived abroad from 1921 to 1932. After his return as a celebrated writer, he became the most important figure in Socialist Realism. On June 18, 1936, Gorky died of influenza, received a solemn funeral and was buried along the Kremlin wall. In the 3rd Moscow Show Trial Gorky's death

played a central role as an alleged murder. Yagoda "confessed" to having ordered the murder of Gorky and his son Max (see below) by arranging for them to be given deliberately incorrect medical treatment.

53 In 1934, Maxim Gorky published the book *Kanal imeni Stalina*, in which a collective of several dozen Soviet poets and writers glorified the construction of the White Sea Canal as a great re-education project. The volume was published in three editions totaling 114,000 copies (one of them in an exquisitely designed edition). After Yagoda's arrest in 1937 and the arrests and shootings of numerous others involved in the volume, the book was confiscated and almost the entire edition was destroyed.

54 Gorky's exact words in his preface to the volume were that the construction of the canal was "an outstandingly successful experiment in the mass transformation of former enemies of the dictatorship of the proletariat into qualified working-class collaborators [*sotrudnikov rabochego klassa*] and even into enthusiasts of work necessary to the state." M. Gor'kii, L. Averbach, and S. Firin, eds., *Belomorsko-Baltiiskii Kanal imeni Stalina. Istoriia stroitel'stva* (Moscow: Gosudarstvennoe izdatel'stvo "Istoriia fabrik i zavodov," 1934), 12.

55 The "Bolshevo Work Commune of the OGPU No. 1" was a residential and work facility operated by the GPU from 1924 to 1937 at the railroad junction of Bolshevo (not Bol'shevo, as given by Evreinov in Russian) for homeless and difficult-to-educate juvenile offenders. Originally designed as an experimental pedagogical project, it quickly became a de facto institution of forced prison labor. Named after Yagoda in the wake of his rise to power, it was dissolved in 1937, after Yagoda's arrest, and its leading staff fell victim to the Great Terror.

56 Most likely, Evreinov took this poem of praise from the young convicts from an article by the former Prime Minister of the Provisional Government of 1917, Aleksandr Kerensky. The latter used it to open his commentary on Yagoda's arrest in the émigré newspaper *Novaia*

Rossiia. See A. Kerensky, "Golos izdaleka," *Novaia Rossiia*, April 11, 1937.

57 In Russian, the shortened form *kontslager'*: A reference to the concentration camps.

58 A rather familial form of address in Russian, using only the patronymic, without the first or last name.

59 In the original, *khoziain russkoi zemli*: Before the revolution, this was one of the titles of the Tsar.

60 In the original, *bezbozhniki* (the godless). This was the self-designation of the representatives of the Soviet anti-religious movement after 1917. The anti-religious campaign was legitimized by Lenin's decree on the separation of church and state and of schools from the church on January 23, 1918. After episodic but quite fierce anti-religious persecutions and agitprop campaigns of the revolutionary and civil war periods, the Union of the Godless (*soiuz bezbozhnikov*) was founded as a mass organization in 1925.

61 *Tukhachevskii, Mikhail Nikolaevich* (1893–1937): General of the Red Army, Marshal of the Soviet Union and Deputy People's Commissar for Defense. From an aristocratic family, he was a career officer in World War I. Joined the Red Army voluntarily and made a career as a successful army commander in the Civil War as well as in the Soviet-Polish War. One of the central Soviet military theorists of the 1920s and 1930s. Appointed Marshal in 1935. He was arrested in May 1937, sentenced to death as part of an alleged military conspiracy along with other leading military officers, and executed on June 11.

62 Radek stayed in Germany during the German Revolution of 1918–1919 and was also imprisoned there for a time.

63 "with a cynicism that approaches grace" (*tsinizm, dochodiashchii do gratsii*): quotation from the poem *Ubogaia i nariadnaia* (1860) by Nikolai Alekseevich Nekrasov, here erroneously attributed to the writer Mikhail Saltykov-Shchedrin.

64 Allusion to the assassination of the last tsar, Nikolai II, and his family in Ekaterinburg on July 17, 1918, carried out in an extremely cruel

manner by local Cheka members with the approval of the party leadership. The process is documented in detail in Mark D. Steinberg and Vladimir M. Khrustalev, *The Fall of the Romanovs: Political Dreams and Personal Struggles in a Time of Revolution* (New Haven: Yale University Press, 1995), 277–366.

65   *Mariengof, Anatolii Borisovich* (1897–1962): Russian writer, belonged to the circle of Imaginists in the 1920s. Had been acquainted with Bukharin since 1918 and was at times sponsored by him. In his autobiographical novel *A Novel without Lies (Roman bez vran'ia)*, published in 1926, he characterizes Bukharin as follows: "His eyes jumped around so merrily that I involuntarily thought: Did he perhaps, before entering the room, play a game of dice [*babki*] in the courtyard [...]? In short, I liked him very much." Evreinov is probably referring to this quote, although he renders it inaccurately. See Anatoly B. Mariengof, *Sobranie sochinenii v trekh tomakh*, vol. 2.1 (Moscow: Izdatel'stvo TERRA, 2013), 504.

66   Evreinov probably took this characterization of Rykov from the German edition of Boris Bazhanov's memoirs (see below): Boris Bajanow, *Stalin, der rote Diktator* (Berlin: Verlag der Paul Aretz G.m.b.H., 1931), 44.

67   In 1924, against fierce opposition, especially from Trotsky and other members of the Left Opposition, the state vodka monopoly, which had been abolished in 1919, was reintroduced in order to—as Trotsky claimed—improve the state budget. The new state-issued vodka was popularly named "Rykovka," but only in "honor" of Rykov as the current chairman of the Soviet government, not because of his alleged reputation as a drinker, since contemporary sources report Rykov's rather restrained consumption of alcohol. Evreinov was apparently guided in this detail by Bazhanov's memoirs, which describe Rykov as consuming alcohol in excess, and note that "The new vodka invented by the Bolsheviks is popularly called 'Rykovka' in honor of Rykov." (Bajanow, *Stalin, der rote Diktator*, 23).

68   In the original: *na Rusi est' vesël'e piti*: quotation from the *Primary Chronicle (Povest' vremennych let)*, the oldest East Slavic chronicle from the 12th century. Such was the answer of Grand Prince Vladimir of Kiev to a Muslim envoy who wanted to convert him and Rus' to Islam.

69   A type of cigarette that emerged in Russia as early as the 19th century, which has no filter but a cardboard mouthpiece that is compressed when smoked, serves as a rudimentary filter and blocks tobacco fibers.

70   As early as the 1st Moscow Trial, it was insinuated that Bukharin and Rykov were "complicit," and this was reported in the newspapers even during the trial, to the great alarm of those involved. See Hedeler, *Nikolai Bucharin*, 427.

71   *Trotskii, Lev Davydovich* (born Bronshtein, 1879–1940): Russian revolutionary, People's Commissar, founder of the Red Army. From a family of farmers, he became active in the revolutionary movement as a youth in southern Russia, fled abroad after internal banishment, and soon rose to become a widely respected socialist publicist. At times he worked closely with Lenin, albeit repeatedly in conflict, but did not join the Bolsheviks until 1917. Already played an important role in the 1905 Revolution, then a central one in the October Revolution of 1917. One of the most important military and civilian politicians of Soviet Russia. Organizer of the "Left Opposition" against Stalin, Zinoviev and Kamenev in 1923–1924, and the "United Opposition" against Stalin with the latter two in 1926–1927. Was finally removed from power in 1927, banished, and forcibly expelled from the country in 1929. Played a central role in organizing an international Communist opposition to Stalin in exile in Turkey, France, Norway, and finally Mexico, excelled as a sharp analyst of Stalinism and international politics. In the Moscow Trials and the Great Terror, Stalin's propaganda turned Trotsky into the epitome of absolute evil and treated him as a de facto absentee chief defendant. Trotsky defended himself against the accusations with an

international campaign, supported by some prominent intellectuals such as John Dewey. He was murdered in Mexico by a Soviet agent in 1940.

72 Quote from a statement by Trotsky on the 2nd Moscow Show Trial, read on February 9, 1937, at a solidarity meeting organized by his supporters in New York and subsequently published in his newspaper, *Biulleten' Oppozitsii*. The full quote reads: "Through the GPU Stalin can trap his victim in an abyss of black despair, humiliation, infamy, in such a manner that he takes upon himself the most monstrous crimes, with the prospect of imminent death or a feeble ray of hope for the future as the sole outcome. If, indeed, he does not contemplate suicide [...]. But do not forget that in the prisons of the GPU even suicide is often an inaccessible luxury!" Leon Trotsky, "I Stake My Life," in *Leon Trotsky Speaks* (New York: Pathfinder, 1972), 373–374.

73 Bukharin was editor-in-chief of *Izvestiia* between May 1934 and January 1937. In view of the public smear campaign against him that had already begun in the summer of 1936, which also took place in "his" newspaper, he refused to continue working in the editorial office as of June 28, 1936, and de facto resigned from editorial work. However, he was listed in the imprint of the newspaper as editor-in-chief until January 16, 1937. See Hedeler, *Chronik*, 82–83, 139; Hedeler, *Nikolai Bucharin*, 425–437.

74 German in the original. A mild swearword.

75 *Lubyanka*: Colloquial name for the headquarters of the Soviet secret police, located on the square of the same name in Moscow. In the basement of the Lubyanka was the central prison of the secret police, where countless prisoners were tortured and executed.

76 Yezhov's nickname, which refers mainly to his diminutive height of 4 feet 10 inches.

77 *Bazhanov, Boris Georgievich* (1900–1982): Soviet party functionary, defector, and memoirist. Joined the Communist Party as a student in 1919, was one of Stalin's personal secretaries 1923–1925. Fled to France in 1928 via Central Asia, Iran and India. Best known for his

polemical exposé book *Memoirs of Stalin's Former Secretary*. In it, Bazhanov exaggerated his actual role within the party bureaucracy and cited numerous incidents and episodes that cannot be verified from other sources, but he also recorded many valuable impressions. For Evreinov, the book seems to have been a central source for his play. The book was published in Paris in 1930 and translated into several languages, yet initially not into English. A Russian edition did not appear in Evreinov's lifetime either. The English translation, *Bazhanov and the Damnation of Stalin* (1990), is based on a massively revised edition, reedited by Bazhanov himself shortly before his death. Thus, here I refer to the 1930 German edition *Stalin, der rote Diktator*, as it is most likely close to the text that Evreinov had before him.

78   This quotation is not found in *Stalin, der rote Diktator*. It may possibly have come from another edition or publication of Bazhanov.

79   In the German edition it says "... that Stalin is only a very uneducated Caucasian, who has no understanding of literature or foreign languages, who not only understands almost nothing of economic and financial affairs, but also can only make sense of most major political problems with difficulty." Bajanow, *Stalin, der rote Diktator*, 17.

80   See ibid., 29.

81   Bazhanov states, "Against these lickspittles Stalin is always very rough. He only respects people who stand up to him." Ibid., 25.

82   *Tovstukha, Ivan Pavlovich* (1889–1935): close confidant of Stalin, his secretary and speechwriter from 1918 to 1935. Died of tuberculosis in 1935.
     Kanner, Grigory Iosifovich (1897–1938): associate in Stalin's secretariat. Was shot in 1938 in the course of the Great Terror.

83   Compare Bajanow, *Stalin, der rote Diktator*, 25.

84   This quote is also not documented in *Stalin, der rote Diktator*.

85   *Kaganovich, Lazar' Moiseevich* (1893–1991): Soviet politician, member of the CC of the VKP(b), for a time general secretary of the CC of the CP of Ukraine. 1934–1935 chairman of the Commission for Party Control, 1935–1937 People's Commissar for Transportation, 1937–1939

People's Commissar for Heavy Industry. Close confidant of Stalin, personally co-responsible for numerous death sentences in the Great Terror. Deposed and expelled from the party under Khrushchev.

86 *Molotov, Viacheslav Mikhailovich* (born Skriabin, 1890–1986): Soviet politician and Stalin's closest confidant. Was a member of the Bolshevik underground, and after the October Revolution he had career in various state and party offices. Member of the CC of the VKP(b). From 1930 to 1941, chairman of the Council of People's Commissars and the Council of Labor and Defense. Later Soviet foreign minister. Also deposed and expelled from the party under Khrushchev.

87 *Chervonets*: Soviet gold-based and internationally traded currency, introduced in 1922.

88 The metaphor of "rabid dogs" for those accused and convicted in the show trials was used throughout the years of the Great Terror and was echoed in slogans, editorials, and propaganda poems. Vyshinsky, who as prosecutor in the 1st Moscow Trial demanded in his closing argument to shoot the "rabid dogs," was probably the first to introduce the phrase. Compare Hedeler, *Chronik*, 78, 107, 382, 390, 394.

89 *Karev, Nikolai Afanas'evich* (1901–1936): Soviet philosopher and party functionary, deputy chairman of the Plan Commission of the Academy of Sciences. Already disgraced by 1933. Accused in the 1st Moscow Trial of complicity in Kirov's murder, arrested and sentenced to death.

90 *Kirov, Sergei Mironovich* (born Kostikov, 1886–1934): Soviet politician, party leader of Leningrad. Was shot by an assassin in 1934. His assassination provided the catalyst for the Stalinist party purges that resulted in the Moscow Trials and the Great Terror. Although the assassin, Leonid Nikolaev, a low-level party official, apparently acted without incitement, he confessed under interrogation to being part of a counterrevolutionary organization led by Kamenev and Zinoviev. For the definitive state of research on the Kirov murder and its aftermath, see Matthew E. Lenoe, *The Kirov Murder and Soviet History* (New Haven: Yale University Press, 2010).

91 *Lunacharskii, Anatolii Vasil'evich* (1875–1933): Russian and Soviet literary critic and playwright, one of the most important cultural officials of the early Soviet Union. 1917–1929 People's Commissar for Education. Lunacharsky died of a heart attack while traveling in France in 1933, so the reference to his "recent" search is an anachronism. Moreover, Lunacharsky never fell out of favor under Stalin and thus had no reason to be searched by the secret police.

92 *Mrachkovskii, Sergei Vital'evich* (1888–1936): Russian revolutionary, Soviet politician and army leader, Left Opposition activist. Sentenced to death in the 1st Moscow Trial and shot.

93 *Smirnov, Ivan Nikitich* (1881–1936): Russian revolutionary, Soviet politician, one of the leaders of the Left Opposition. Sentenced to death in the 1st Moscow Trial and shot.

94 This radio speech could not be connected to a specific text from the time of the Moscow Trials. It is conceivable that Evreinov wrote it himself, especially since it has some turns of phrase that are rather atypical of Stalinist propaganda in the 1930s.

95 *"close unity ..."*: this part of the radio speech is not in the present text. It is possible that the speech was abbreviated, but this was not taken note of in the stage direction.

96 The suspicion that Yagoda had collaborated with the tsarist secret police as a young revolutionary was repeatedly raised throughout history, but has never been substantiated—not even after the archives were opened after the end of the USSR. Among other things, defected NKVD agent Walter Krivitsky, in his 1939 tell-all book *In Stalin's Secret Service* published in the West, argued that Yezhov had made this accusation against Yagoda at a closed conference of leading NKVD operatives in early 1937, thus initiating his persecution. It is likely that Evreinov knew Krivitsky's book. On Yagoda's biography, see A. L. Litvin, "Genrikh Iagoda. Ot anarkho-kommunizma k Gulagu," in *Genrikh Iagoda. Narkom vnutrennikh del SSSR, General'nyi komissar gosudarstvennoi bezopasnosti. Sbornik dokumentov*, ed. by V. K. Vinogradov (Kazan': s.n., 1997), 21–45, esp. 31.

97   In the original: *ochranka*. The Russian word is the colloquial name
     of the secret police in Tsarist Russia, whose full title was "Division
     for the Defense of Public Security and Order" (Russian: *Otdelenie po
     okhraneniiu obshchestvennoi bezopasnosti i poriadka*).

98   In Gorky's story "Byvshie liudi" ("Those Who Were," 1897) about the
     merchant Ivan Petunnikov it says: "Cursed crossbreed of fox and
     pig!" In his indictment speech of March 11, 1938, Vyshinsky, also
     citing Gorky, refers to Bukharin as a "damnable cross of a fox and a
     swine." (*Report of Court Proceedings in the Case of the Anti-Soviet Bloc
     of Rights and Trotskyites*, 685.

99   *Dzerzhinskii, Feliks Edmundovich* (1877–1926): Polish revolutionary
     and Soviet politician. Founder and, between 1917 and 1926, first
     head of the Cheka secret police (later GPU).

100 This saying is attributed to Stalin by Boris Souvarine, a leading func-
     tionary of the CP of France who spent much time in Moscow in the
     early 1920s socializing with Soviet leaders but was expelled from the
     party in 1924 as a supporter of Trotsky. In 1935, he published the
     first major and critical biography of Stalin in France, which is still
     considered a milestone today. It states that Stalin said this to Ka-
     menev and Dzerzinsky in a "frank conversation" in 1923. See Boris
     Souvarine, *Staline. Aperçu historique du bolchévisme* [1935] (Paris:
     Les Éditions Gérard Lebovici, 1985), 448. However, Evreinov may
     not have read the biography, which was never translated into Rus-
     sian, but only its review in the Russian émigré journal *Novyi grad*,
     where the quotation is translated from French into Russian exactly
     as it then appears in the original Russian text of *The Steps of Nem-
     esis*. Compare Georgy P. Fedotov, "BORIS SOUVARINE. Staline,"
     Novyi grad, no. 10 (1935): 142–144.

101 In the original, *Kradek*: pun, based on the Polish word for "thief."
     This is how Radek sometimes jokingly signed his pre-revolution-
     ary letters, and this is also how he was occasionally disparagingly
     dubbed by his opponents within Social Democracy. In addition, in
     1910, as a member of the SKDPiL, one of several Polish Social Demo-

cratic parties, Radek was falsely accused of stealing from comrades by its rival party, the PPS. See Jean-François Fayet, *Karl Radek (1885–1939). Biographie politique* (Bern et al.: Lang, 2004), 61ff, 72, 189.

102 French telephone model also common in early 20th century Russia.

103 *Piatakov, Iuri (Georgii) Leonidovich* (1890–1937): Soviet party and state functionary, chairman of the State Bank administration. Member of the CC of the VKP(b), Deputy People's Commissar for Heavy Industry. At times active in the Left Opposition. Sentenced to death in the 2nd Moscow Trial and shot.

104 *Sokol'nikov, Grigorii Iakovlevich* (born Girsh Brilliant, 1888–1939). Early Bolshevik and Soviet party and state radio official. Candidate of the CC of the VKP(b), First Deputy of the People's Commissar for Forestry. At times active in the United Opposition. Sentenced to ten years in prison in the 2nd Moscow Trial and killed in his cell by the NKVD in 1939, just like Radek (see above).

105 Tukhachevsky's co-defendants in the trial of the Red Army leadership in June 1937:

Gamarnik, Ian Borisovich (1894–1937): Soviet party and military politician, head of the Red Army political administration. Committed suicide while awaiting arrest.

Iakir, Iona Emmanuilovich (1896–1937): senior Soviet military leader, commander of the Kiev Military District. He and the following two individuals were arrested as part of an alleged military conspiracy, sentenced to death on June 11, 1937, and shot the following day.

Uborevich, Ieronim Petrovich (1896–1937): candidate of the CC of the VKP(b) and high-ranking Soviet military leader. Chief of the Belarusian military district.

Kork, Avgust Ivanovich (1887–1937): Soviet army commander and diplomat. Director of the military academy.

106 A famous statement about Stalin by Lenin. First appeared in a February 1913 letter from Lenin to Maxim Gorky, in which he wrote: "We have a fine Georgian here who [...] is writing a great article for which he has collected all the Austrian and other data." L. Kamenev, ed.,

Lenins Briefe an Gorki. 1908–1913 (Vienna: Verlag für Literatur und Politik, 1924), letter 24.

107 After the October Revolution, the 2nd Congress of Soviets on October 25 (November 7), 1917, initially abolished the death penalty, although the Bolsheviks were divided on the issue. However, it was reinstated by decree on February 21, 1918. Evreinov may be referring to Radek's article "Krasnyi terror" in *Izvestiia*, September 6, 1918, in which he advocates public shootings with the participation of the "masses." See Nikita Petrov, "Group Picture of Soviet Assassins. The Trajectory of Stalinist Executioners from the Revolution to the Great Terror," *Connexe: les espaces postcommunistes en question(s)* 5 (2019): 155–178, https://doi.org/10.5077/journals/connexe.2019. e257, here 157–158.

108 *Dem'ian Bednyi* (real name Efim Alekseevich Pridvorov, 1883–1945): Soviet poet, one of the best-known propagandists of the Bolsheviks in the first decades after the Revolution. His pseudonym "Bednyi" means "poor man."

109 The second constitution of the USSR was adopted on December 5, 1936, replacing the 1924 constitution. It had the appearance of being democratic, of guaranteeing human rights and general elections with secret ballots. There is a wide historiographical debate about the meaning and purpose of this constitution. Among the Stalin regime's reasons for adopting such a "democratic" constitution was enhancing the regime's prestige abroad in line with the Comintern's "popular front" strategy (see below), as well as to create the appearance of democratization internally, since the adoption of the constitution was accompanied by a staged public debate campaign. See, among others, Aleksandr V. Shubin, "Narodnyi front. Izmenenie v strategii Stalina," in *Rossiia i mir glazami drug druga. Iz istorii vzaimootnoshenii*, ed. by Aleksandr V. Golubev, vol. 4 (Moscow: IRI RAN, 2007), 106–126; Samantha Lomb, *Stalin's Constitution: Soviet Participatory Politics and the Discussion of the 1936 Draft Constitution* (Abingdon: Routledge, 2018).

110 Stalin's draft constitution involved numerous leading Bolsheviks who would fall victim to Stalin's terror only a short time later, including Bukharin, Radek, and Sokol'nikov. See Hedeler, *Nikolai Bucharin*, 406–413.

111 *Braude, Il'ia Davidovich* (1885–1955): prominent Soviet lawyer who acted as defense counsel in various show trials, including the 2nd and 3rd Moscow Trials. In his memoirs, published 19 years after his death, he omits the period of Stalin's terror. In the 3rd Moscow Trial, Braude characterized Levin in his defense speech as "very wishy-washy" and "inclined towards panic" to explain why Levin had not resisted Yagoda's alleged orders to poison people. See *Report of Court Proceedings in the Case of the Anti-Soviet Bloc of Rights and Trotskyites*, 700.

112 *Quantum satis* (Latin): "sufficient quantity".

113 *Menzhinskii, Viacheslav Rudolfovich* (1874–1934): Polish revolutionary and Soviet politician. Leader of the OGPU from 1926 to 1934, Yagoda's predecessor in this position. Fell severely ill and was bedridden in the last years of his life, so that Yagoda became the de facto head of the OGPU even before his death. In the 3rd Moscow Trial, Yagoda pleaded guilty to having arranged false medical treatment for Menzhinsky and thus to having killed him on behalf of the "Bloc of Rights and Trotskyites".

114 At the trial, Levin stated that he had been subdued by Yagoda over a long period of time with expensive gifts, including lavish bouquets of flowers and very good French wines. See *Report of Court Proceedings in the Case of the Anti-Soviet Bloc of Rights and Trotskyites*, 514.

115 *Saltykov-Shchedrin, Mikhail Evgrafovich* (1826–1889): Russian writer and satirist. His name is written incorrectly in the original, perhaps intentionally by Evreinov to characterize Yagoda's education.

116 In Saltykov-Shchedrin's cycle of stories *Pompadury i pompadurshi* (1863–1873), there is a caricature of a "liberal" provincial governor whose liberalism amounts to superficialities and gestures. This figure was evoked by Radek during the struggle of the inner-party opposition to Stalin in a speech at the Communist Academy to ridicule

Stalin and his idea of "socialism in one country"—which Stalin again opposed in a speech in 1926. See J. V. Stalin, *Concerning Questions of Leninism* in *Works*, vol. 8 (Moscow: Foreign Languages Publishing House, 1954), 64.

117 Word play on the meaning of Gorky's pseudonym (real name Aleksei Maksimovich Peshkov): the "bitter one."

118 *Maksim Peshkov* (1897–1934): son of the writer Maxim Gorky and his first wife. Died suddenly in 1934 after a short illness, officially of pneumonia.

119 According to several contemporary witnesses, Yagoda was in love with the wife of Gorky's son, the artist Nadezhda "Timosha" Peshkova, and stalked her repeatedly after her husband's death. This may be the reason for the remarkable break in Yagoda's interrogation during the trial when it comes to the murder of "Max": At this point, in taciturn manner and in sharp contrast to the dramaturgy of the trial, Yagoda insisted that she had committed the murder for personal motives and refused to give any further testimony about it. See *Report of Court Proceedings in the Case of the Anti-Soviet Bloc of Rights and Trotskyites*, 573.

120 *Maliuta Skuratov* (?-1573): notorious member of the *oprichniki*, the closest companions of Tsar Ivan IV the Terrible. Headed the secret police department and personally carried out extraordinarily cruel tortures on opponents of the tsar.

121 A fictitious person.

122 *Popular Front*: name given to the alliances of left-wing and left-bourgeois parties that formed the government in France (Front populaire, until 1937) and Spain (Frente Popular, until 1939) from 1936. In 1935, at its 7th World Congress, the Comintern had moved away from the previously valid "social fascism thesis," according to which social democracy represented the "left wing of fascism," and had called for communist parties abroad to form alliances with social democratic and left-bourgeois forces. While the new Soviet strategy initially received much encouragement in anti-fascist circles abroad,

enthusiasm was already dampened by the Moscow Trials. The Stalin-Hitler Pact of 1939 finally put an end to the Popular Front strategy.

123 *Brik, Osip Maksimovich* (1888–1945): Soviet avant-garde writer and literary critic, important theorist of Formalism. Brik had a legal education and worked in the legal department of the Petrograd Cheka from 1920. However, he was dismissed from the Cheka as early as 1923 and, of course, was not active as an NKVD torturer at the time of the Great Terror.

124 A fictitious person. No archbishop by this name has been identified.

125 In 1922–1924, a struggle raged within the Russian Orthodox Church between the supporters of its head, an opponent of the Bolsheviks, Patriarch Tikhon (1865–1925), and the representatives of the "Living Church," also called the "Renovationists" (*obnovlentsy*), who demanded ecclesiastical reforms and recognition of the Bolsheviks. The "Renovationists" were supported by the Bolsheviks in order to weaken the church as a whole, but were dropped quite quickly. In the late 1930s, the disputes between the Tikhonites and the Renovationists were no longer relevant, as clergy of both tendencies were equally persecuted. It was not until World War II that the church in the Soviet Union was again given more leeway, with the regime opting to support the former Tikhon camp.

126 *RCP*: abbreviation for the Russian Communist Party (*Rossiiskaia Kommunisticheskaia Partiia*). However, it was renamed VKP(b) (*Vsesoiuznaia Kommunisticheskaia Partiia*, "All-Union Communist Party") as early as 1925.

127 *Komsomol*: short for: *Kommunisticheskii soiuz molodëzhi* ("Communist Youth League"). Youth organization of the Communist Party.

128 *NKGB*: abbreviation for *Narodnyi komissariat gosudarstvennoi bezopasnosti*, the People's Commissariat for State Security. The successor institution of the NKVD was established only in 1941. This anachronism shows that Evreinov was probably still working on the piece at least in the early 1940s.

129 Quote from the poem *Pesnia narodu* ("Song to the People," 1936) by the Kazakh folk poet Dzhambul Dzhabaev (1846–1945), who wrote numerous odes to Stalin and other high party officials, including Nikolai Ezhov.

130 A youth organization for 10–15 year-olds that was part of the Komsomol.

131 Abbreviation for the full name of the Komsomol, "Rossiiskii leninskii kommunisticheskii soiuz molodezhi" ("Russian Communist Lenin Association of Youth"). However, the abbreviation had already been replaced by VLKSM in 1926 in keeping with the analogous renaming of the Communist Party.

132 Popular textbook on the principles of communism written in 1919 by Bukharin and Evgeny Preobrazhensky. By the late 1930s, however, it was long out of circulation.

133 Evreinov's staging of the "Red Baptism" largely coincides with surviving instructions for this ritual from the early 1920s; see for example O. M. Beliaeva, "'Krasnaia' obriadnost' kak instrument politicheskogo vospitaniia sovetskikh grazhdan," *Arkhivy Sankt-Peterburga*, n.d., https://spbarchives.ru/cgaipd_publications/-/asset_publisher/yV5V/content/id/668135. The only element that clearly distinguishes Evreinov's description from the 1920s is that his "Red Baptism" takes place in a private room, which would not have been typical for the 1920s. In any case, "Red Baptisms" were hardly practiced anymore by the 1930s.

134 *Vesëlye rebiata* (*The Merry Boys*) was a movie musical directed by Grigory Alexandrov in 1934. The film and the songs from it, especially the march, were tremendously popular.

135 The Ryabushinsky family was a rich industrialist family of peasant origin in pre-revolutionary Russia, known as patrons and collectors of art.

136 Poem by Dem'ian Bednyi published in 1936 on a propaganda poster (design: B.V. Iordanskii). See http://redavantgarde.com/collection/show-collection/1600-we-have-they-have-.html. Evreinov has combined several fragments from the original.

137 Most likely a fictitious person.

138 A well-known patriotic song, written for the 1936 musical *Circus* directed by Grigory Alexandrov.

139 After Bukharin's and Rykov's names were dropped in the 1ˢᵗ Moscow Trial (see above), a cross-examination of both was arranged with Sokol'nikov, which took place in the presence of Kaganovich, Ezhov and Vyshinskii on September 8, 1936. Bukharin and Rykov denied the accusations made by Sokol'nikov and demanded a denial in *Pravda*. This was actually printed on September 10, and Stalin personally reassured Bukharin. Meanwhile, however, more compromising statements against him were collected even after this reassurance. See Hedeler, *Chronik*, 90–91.

140 Well-known saying attributed to Lev Tolstoy. This is said to have been his reaction to the writing style of the Russian Expressionist writer Leonid Andreev (1871–1919).

141 *Bezymenskii, Aleksandr Il'ich* (1898–1974): Soviet poet, dramaturge, and Komsomol official. A one-time protégé of Trotsky, he was initially a supporter of the Left Opposition but quickly moved away from it and later condemned the victims of the Moscow Trials. *The Shot*, a play in verse, dates from 1929 and critiques bureaucratization. The play was controversial, partly because it contained a direct attack on Mikhail Bulgakov, and partly because it allowed for "anti-party" readings. Bezymensky personally appealed to Stalin, who acquitted him of the latter charge. See Lev Kolodnyo, "'Vystrel' poeta Bezymenskogo," *Moskovskii komsomolets*, May 30, 2019, https://www.mk.ru/social/2019/05/30/vystrel-poeta-bezymenskogo.html. Interestingly, it was the émigré press that interpreted the monologue Evreinov quoted as a caricature of Stalin and his regime; the quotes cited here were printed by the Paris émigré newspaper *Vozrozhdenie* (Aug. 18, 1929, p. 2) under the headline "Portrait of Stalin" with a commentary. It is conceivable that Evreinov, who by then was no longer living in the Soviet Union, quoted the passages after this publication.

142 The Russian folk song is about a little goat that lives with an old woman and one day runs away into the forest, where it is eaten by wolves, after which all that is left of it are horns and bones. The protagonists modify the last verse of the song, replacing the kid with Stalin.

143 This and the following part of the radio speech together with the poem could not be sourced to a specific text from the time of the Moscow Trials. It is conceivable that Evreinov wrote it himself, especially since it has some phrases that are rather atypical for Stalinist propaganda, such as "long-suffering fatherland."

144 Nemesis: in Greek mythology, the goddess of righteous anger and retributive justice.

145 See above.

146 Russian proverb. In the original: *na lovtsa i zver' bezhit.*

147 In the original: *kot naplakal*, literally "[as the] cat has wept [tears]". A Russian turn of phrase that means a very small amount of nothing.

148 A detention prison in Moscow, built in the 18th century, one of the oldest and most notorious Russian prisons still in operation. During Stalin's time, numerous people sentenced to camp imprisonment were held at Butyrka before they were transferred elsewhere. During the Great Terror, Butyrka, which was equipped for 1,000 prisoners, housed up to 25,000 detainees, and cells designed for 25 prisoners at times held up to 170 inmates.

149 IZO is the abbreviation for Russian *izoliator*, a prison with solitary confinement used to investigate suspected criminals. Evreinov probably does not mean a concrete, historically verified prison here. Radek himself was in fact imprisoned in the Lubyanka. Fayet, *Karl Radek*, 704.

150 Radek's co-defendants in the 2nd Moscow Trial. All sentenced to death. *Nikolai Ivanovich Muralov* (1877–1937) was a prominent party and military official of the 1920s, as was *Yakov Naumovich Drobnis* (1890–1937). *Alexei Aleksandrovich Shestov* (1896–1937) was a functionary in the Siberian mining industry. *Mikhail Solomo-novich Boguslavskii* (1886–1937) was a party functionary. *Stanislav*

Antonovich Rataichak (1894–1937) was an economic functionary in the chemical industry. *Leonid Petrovich Serebriakov* (1888–1937) was an old Bolshevik and functionary in Soviet transportation. With the exceptions of Shestov and Rataichak, all were former leading members of the Left Opposition.

151 *Sedov, Lev L'vovich* (1906–1938): Trotsky's son, one of his closest political collaborators and supporters in exile. Engaged in active organizational and journalistic opposition to Stalinism and the show trials. He published, among other works, the "Red Book on the Moscow Trial," (published in Russian, French and German in 1936). He was closely monitored by Soviet intelligence and his closest collaborator, Mark Zborovsky, was an agent of Stalin. Sedov died on February 16, 1938, in a Paris hospital after an appendectomy. Whether he was murdered remains unclear. See Bertrand M. Patenaude, *Trotsky: Downfall of a Revolutionary* (New York: Harper Perennial, 2010), 114–115.

152 A fabricated accusation. In reality, Trotsky and his son had only contempt for Radek since the latter had stabbed the Left Opposition in the back. During the 1st Moscow Trial, Sedov, in a letter to his father, referred to Radek as "a scoundrel crawling on his belly for almost 10 years" (Hedeler, *Chronik*, 75.).

153 German in the original. Correct spelling: "Missverständnis," meaning "misunderstanding".

154 Polish in the original, written in Russian script. Meaning "Little Marshal".

155 In the original, a word written in Russian using a Polish word, from Polish *chować się*: "To hide oneself".

156 Polish in the original, written in Russian script. Meaning "I beg you"/"I am asking you".

157 Polish in the original, written in Russian script. Meaning: "Whether it is so, or whether it is not".

158 *Ludendorff, Erich Friedrich Wilhelm* (1865–1937): German general in the First World War. Allowed Lenin to pass through Germany because he hoped it would destabilize Russia.

159 *Platten, Fritz* (1883–1942): Swiss Social Democratic and later Communist politician. Organized Lenin's return trip from Switzerland to Russia after the February Revolution of 1917. Emigrated to the Soviet Union in 1923. Sentenced to camp imprisonment in 1938, shot on April 22, 1942 (Lenin's birthday).

160 Fritz Platten, *Die Reise Lenins durch Deutschland im plombierten Wagen* ("Lenin's Journey through Germany in an Armored Car") (Berlin: Neuer Deutscher Verlag, 1924). Platten describes (pp. 27–28) that, at Radek's suggestion, the Swiss correspondent of the *Frankfurter Zeitung* proposed the idea of transporting Lenin from Switzerland to Russia to the German embassy in Bern. The book also includes a contribution by Radek himself ("Im plombierten Wagen durch Deutschland," pp. 62–66), in which, however, he does not claim to have personally convinced Ludendorff to make the trip, but instead recounts the same story with the journalist and the German embassy.

161 Quotation from the memoirs of the former Bolshevik and confidant of Lenin, Vladimir Voytinsky (1885–1960), who, in his memoirs published in 1924 in emigration, cites a saying by Lenin from a personal conversation: "The party is not a boarding house for noble maidens. Party workers must not be judged by the narrow standards of bourgeois morality. Sometimes a scoundrel can be useful to us precisely because he is a scoundrel." *Gody pobed i porazhenii*, vol. 2 (Berlin: Izdatel'stvo Grzhebina, 1924), 102.

162 A quote from Lenin's work *Left-Wing Communism—An Infantile Disorder* (1920), where it says: "We must be able to stand up to all this, agree to make any sacrifice, and even—if need be—resort to various stratagems, artifices and illegal methods, to evasions and subterfuges, as long as we get into the trade unions, remain in them and carry on communist work within them at all costs." *Works*, vol. 31 (Moscow: Progress Publishers, 1966), 55.

163 *Krestinskii, Nikolai Nikolaevich* (1883–1938): Russian revolutionary, Soviet state functionary and diplomat, People's Commissar for Finance 1918–1922, then diplomat in Germany. Supporter of the Left

and United Opposition. At the 3rd Moscow Trial, the only defendant to initially deny his guilt publicly. Nevertheless, sentenced to death.

164 *Rakovskii, Khristian Georgievich* (1873–1941). Bulgarian and Romanian revolutionary, Soviet party official, and diplomat. Trotsky's long-time close friend, supporter of the Left and United Opposition. Sentenced to twenty years imprisonment in the 3rd Moscow Trial. Shot in 1941.

165 Defendants in the 3rd Moscow Trial.

Chernov, Mikhail Aleksandrovich (1891–1938): member of the CC of the VKP(b), People's Commissar for Agriculture. Sentenced to death.

Rozengol'ts, Arkadii Pavlovich (1889–1938): People's Commissar for Foreign Trade. Sentenced to death.

Bessonov, Sergei Alekseevich (1892–1941): diplomat. Sentenced to 15 years imprisonment, shot in 1941.

Grin'ko, Grigorii Fedorovich (1890–1938): People's Commissar for Finance. Sentenced to death.

Sharangovich, Vasilii Fomich (1897–1938): member of the Central Control Commission, First Secretary of the CC of the CP of Belarus. Sentenced to death.

Khodzhaev, Faizulla Ubaidullaevich (1896–1938): chairman of the Council of People's Commissars of the Uzbek SSR. Sentenced to death.

Ikramov, Akmal Ikramovich (1898–1938): First secretary of the CC of the CP of Uzbekistan. As late as 1937, himself a leading participant in the Great Terror in Uzbekistan. Sentenced to death.

Maksimov-Dikovsky, Veniamin Adamovich (1900–1938): head of department in the People's Commissariat for Transport. Sentenced to death.

Kriuchkov, Petr Petrovich (1889–1938): publishing employee, personal secretary of Maxim Gorky. Sentenced to death.

Pletnev, Dmitri Dmitrievich (1872–1941): professor of medicine, internationally renowned cardiologist, treated Lenin, among others. Sentenced to 25 years imprisonment, shot in 1941.

Kazakov, Ignatii Nikolaevich (1891–1938): physician, specialist in metabolic diseases. Sentenced to death.

166 During the interrogation of Bulanov, who is said to have carried out the attempted poisoning of Yezhov, there is a mention of the "office and [...] rooms which adjoined the office in the building of the People's Commissariat of Internal Affairs which Nikolai Ivanovich Yezhov was to occupy," and of the "spraying of the office which Yezhov was to occupy and the adjoining rooms, the rugs, carpets and curtains" *Report of Court Proceedings in the Case of the Anti-Soviet Bloc of Rights and Trotskyites*, 559.

167 Here Evreinov has lifted two passages from Bukharin's interrogation at the 3ʳᵈ Moscow Trial on March 7, 1938 almost verbatim. The transcript reads: "VYSHINSKY: I am not asking you about conversation in general, but about this conversation. BUKHARIN: In Hegel's "Logic" [*sic!*] the word "this" is considered to be the most difficult word ... VYSHINSKY: I ask the Court to explain to the accused Bukharin that he is here not in the capacity of a philosopher, but a criminal, and he would do better to refrain from talking here about Hegel's philosophy, it would be better first of all for Hegel's philosophy ... BUKHARIN: A philosopher may be a criminal. VYSHINSKY: Yes, that is to say, those who imagine themselves to be philosophers turn out to be spies. Philosophy is out of place here." (*Report of Court Proceedings in the Case of the Anti-Soviet Bloc of Rights and Trotskyites*, 421.) A little earlier, Vyshinsky had admonished the defendant: "VYSHINSKY: Can you answer me without philosophy? BUKHARIN: This is not philosophy. VYSHINSKY: Without philosophical twists and turns." (*Report of Court Proceedings in the Case of the Anti-Soviet Bloc of Rights and Trotskyites*, 400.)

168 "Left Communists": oppositional current founded in early 1918 within the Russian Communist Party around Nikolai Bukharin,

which criticized Lenin's policies and, in particular, the conclusion of the Peace Treaty of Brest-Litovsk from a radically leftist position. As early as the summer of 1918, the "Left Communists" abandoned their positions and ceased their activities. Not identical with the "Left Opposition" of 1923–1924 around Lev Trotsky.

169 At the trial, Bukharin was accused of having planned, as head of the "Left Communists" in 1918, not only to arrest Lenin, Stalin, and Sverdlov, but also to have them assassinated. Bukharin presented the arrest plans as mere talk, but consistently denied the assassination plan, even when confronted with former "Left Communists" who claimed otherwise. See *Report of Court Proceedings in the Case of the Anti-Soviet Bloc of Rights and Trotskyites*, 393.

170 Infamous article in the RSFSR Criminal Code on "counterrevolutionary activity." The article was open to broad interpretation and served as a basis for sentencing political prisoners.

171 Bukharin's popular exposition of the Communists' political program, published in 1918, states, "Like every state, the proletarian state is an organization of the ruling class (since the ruling class here is the working class) and an organization of violence, but violence over the bourgeoisie as a means of defending ourselves from the bourgeoisie and defeating it." Nikolai Ivanovich Bukharin, *Programma kommunistov (bol'shevikov)* (Samara: Tip. Sovnarkhoza, 1919), 14.

172 In Bukharin's text, the relevant passage reads: "Anyone who is afraid of such violence is no revolutionary at all." Ibid.

173 Bukharin had already resigned from the Politburo in 1929, so it is not clear what Evreinov is referring to.

174 In traditional Russian usage, a "dog's death" refers to the death of a sinner who has not had confession.

175 At the 3rd Moscow Trial, Bukharin vehemently denied some of the accusations made against him in the interrogation, especially regarding spying for foreign powers and plotting assassinations against other Soviet leaders. Vyshinsky's strategy against this was to have

some of Bukharin's close party colleagues, above all Rykov, make the corresponding accusations as witnesses.

176 Radek, who had already been convicted in the 2nd Moscow Trial, was not called as a witness for the 3rd Moscow Trial, although he was still alive at that time.

177 In the original, Polish in Russian script. Meaning: "whether, or".

178 *Cherviakov, Aleksandr Grigor'evich* (1892–1937): Belarusian revolutionary, chairman of the Central Executive Committee of the USSR. Committed suicide in 1937.

Goloded, Nikolai Matveevich (1894–1937): secretary of the CC of the CP of Belarus. Expelled from the party and arrested in 1937, jumped from a window during interrogation and died.

Sharangovich: see above.

179 Bukharin vehemently denied the accusation of having spied for foreign powers during the course of the trial itself, even in his closing statement. See *Report of Court Proceedings in the Case of the Anti-Soviet Bloc of Rights and Trotskyites*, 767.

180 Bukharin could hardly have made such a statement. For one thing, it was he who, as late as 1936, on the occasion of his transit through Germany, admonished Stalin amicably that the Soviet Union should devote itself even more to analyzing and combating fascism. See Hermann Weber et al, eds., *Deutschland, Russland, Komintern. Bd. 2: Dokumente (1918–1943). Nach der Archivrevolution: Neuerschlossene Quellen zu der Geschichte der KPD und den deutsch-russischen Beziehungen* (Berlin: De Gruyter, 2015), 1207–1209.

181 In addition to Hegel, Bukharin invoked Spinoza, among others, during the course of the trial. See *Report of Court Proceedings in the Case of the Anti-Soviet Bloc of Rights and Trotskyites*, 394.

182 In the original, *arkharovtsy*: A colloquial expression for policemen, after police commissioner Nikolai Petrovich Arkharov (1742–1797), who was known as the strict commander of the Moscow police in the time of Catherine II.

183   For all the other cruelties used by the NKVD against pretrial detain-
      ees, and despite the experiments of the secret police with poisons
      and other substances for which there are eyewitness accounts, noth-
      ing is known as to whether any psychotropic substances were used
      to influence the defendants of the Moscow Trials. Interestingly,
      Bukharin himself referred to this possibility in his closing remarks:
      "Repentence is often attributed to diverse and absolutely absurd
      things like Thibetan powders and the like. I must say of myself that
      in prison, where I was confined for over a year, I worked, studied,
      and retained my clarity of mind. This will serve to refute by facts all
      fables and absurd counter-revolutionary tales." (*Report of Court Pro-
      ceedings in the Case of the Anti-Soviet Bloc of Rights and Trotskyites*,
      777.)

184   In fact, Yagoda fought at the front in World War I until he was
      wounded and demobilized in late 1916 (see Litvin, "Genrikh Ia-
      goda," 22.) There was no mention of his baptism (Yagoda, who was
      born into a Jewish family, was actually baptized Orthodox pro forma
      in 1913 to circumvent the ban on Jews settling in St. Petersburg) dur-
      ing his questioning at the show trial.

185   Up to this point, Bulanov's testimony is almost identical to his actual
      testimony at the trial. See *Report of Court Proceedings in the Case of
      the Anti-Soviet Bloc of Rights and Trotskyites*, 559.

186   This statement by Bulanov is almost identical to his actual testi-
      mony at the trial. See *Report of Court Proceedings in the Case of the
      Anti-Soviet Bloc of Rights and Trotskyites*, 567.

187   *Abramov-Mirov, Aleksandr Lazarevich* (1895–1937): head of the OMS,
      the Comintern's own foreign intelligence service. Arrested in 1937,
      originally intended as a central defendant in a major show trial of Co-
      mintern operatives. He was accused of funneling money to Trotsky
      through OMS channels. The show trial did not materialize, but he
      was sentenced to death in a secret trial and shot in November 1937.
      See Bernhard H. Bayerlein and Peter Huber, "Protokolle des Terrors
      II. A. L. Abramov-Mirov und V. G. Knorin in Verhörprotokollen des

NKVD," *The International Newsletter of Historical Studies on Comin-tern, Communism and Stalinism* 4/5, no. 9–13 (1997): 216–229; Rein hard Müller, "Der Antikomintern-Block. Prozeßstruktur und Opfer-perspektive," *Utopie Kreativ*, no. 81/82 (1997): 82–95.

The notes are written by Gleb J. Albert, Eric Christen and Monika Ertl.

Sylvia Sasse

The Confession of the Theater
Nikolai Evreinov's "Restaging" of the Moscow Show Trials

The political show trials of the 1930s in the Soviet Union were highly elaborate theatrical productions. High-ranking political leaders confessed to incredible crimes against the Soviet Union: treason, sabotage, espionage, and murder. But in Evreinov's play *The Steps of Nemesis*, it is the organizers of the Moscow show trials themselves who confess. They confess to a different kind of crime: the political theater which they create. "I have been wearing a *mask* all my life, pretending to be a Bolshevik, and I never was! [...] And I'm not the only one who *played a role*, but almost everyone, starting with Stalin ..." as Genrikh Yagoda reveals at the very end of the play.[1]

In the reality of Soviet life at the time, Yagoda, who was the head of the Soviet Ministry of Internal Affairs (NKVD) from 1934 to 1936, would never have said such a thing. He was replaced in 1937 by Nikolai Ezhov, who had been gathering "evidence" against him for some time, and was himself on trial in the third and final public show trial. While Evreinov has Yagoda confess to his play-acting as a Bolshevik in *Nemesis*, the real Yagoda confessed during the historical Moscow show trial to having poisoned his predecessor Viacheslav Menzhinsky as well as the writer Maxim Gorky. He was sentenced to "death by firing squad" on the basis of this confession.

---

1   Nikolai Evreinov, *The Steps of Nemesis*, 138. Emphasis in the original.

Evreinov's play, as can be observed from the scene mentioned above, is not a piece of historically verified documentary theater, nor a factographic reconstruction of events, nor a chronicle of the show trials in the conventional sense, even though Evreinov chooses the subtitle "A Dramatic Chronicle in Six Scenes from Party Life in the USSR (1936–1938)." It is rather a document of contemporary speculation. Evreinov was not alone at the time in asking the questions which his play attempts to answer. What was the purpose of all this memorized, and media-orchestrated staging of political betrayal? Why the staging of guilt, remorse and confession and avowal in the form of the show trials?

Evreinov had not been in Russia for more than ten years, since 1924, when he began working on the play; he was in exile in Paris, writing "for the drawer."[2] In Paris, as his wife Anna Kashina-Evreinova describes in her note, he read everything he could get his hands on about the Moscow show trials: the transcripts in the daily newspapers, the reading of which became "an almost deranged obsession"[3] for him, and the volume *Report of Court Proceedings in the Case of the Anti-Soviet Bloc of Rights and Trotskyites* (*Sudebnyi otchet po delu anti-sovetskogo 'pravo-trockistskogo' bloka*) of the 3rd Trial, published in Moscow. Kashina-Evreinova also reports that he asked the Russian Social Democratic publicist-in-exile Pavel Berlin for advice in assessing the protocols. Evreinov also carefully filed newspaper clippings in folders and labelled them "Theater and Scaffold"; in another folder, dated December 6, 1930, to March 21, 1938, he collects

---

2   Anna Kashina-Evreinova, "In Place of a Preface," in: Evreinov, *Steps of Nemesis*, 7.
3   Ibid.

specific materials on the show trials, including individuals such as Bukharin.[4]

What Evreinov collected and read at that time, however, were transcripts of the show trials that had already undergone a round of censorship. Only after the collapse of the Soviet Union were researchers able to access the unpublished original transcripts and see how passages had been deleted and statements had been completely deleted or rewritten.[5] The basic fact of censorship, however, could already be guessed from the translations of the protocols. The German translation of the third trial, for example, is somewhat more detailed than the Russian original, and some passages are even missing in the Russian, from Nikolai Bukharin's cross-examination in particular. The historian Wladislaw Hedeler, who published a chronicle of the show trials in 2003, emphasizes that to this day it is essentially impossible to ascertain what happened behind the scenes of the show trials. There are "no archive-based source editions that provide information about the preparation, execution and follow-up of the three show trials [...]. The archives where the related documents are kept [...] are inaccessible or largely closed to foreign and Russian researchers."[6]

When Evreinov was writing his play in the 1930s and 1940s almost nothing known today could be proven. In this

4   The articles and sketches collected by Evreinov between 1928 and 1944, the folders, "Teatr i Eshafot," are held in the Russian State Archive of Literature and Art (RGALI), f. 982 (Evreinov), op. 1, ed. khr. 302.

5   See Wladislaw Hedeler, "Ezhov's Scenario for the Great Terror and the Falsified Record of the Third Show Trial," in *Stalin's Terror. High Politics and Mass Repression in the Soviet Union*, ed. by Barry McLoughlin and Kevin McDermott (Basingstoke: Palgrave Macmillan, 2004), 34–55.

6   Wladislaw Hedeler, *Chronik der Moskauer Schauprozesse 1936, 1937 und 1938. Planung, Inszenierung und Wirkung* (Berlin: Akademie Verlag 2003), XXVII.

respect, Evreinov's play also documents the rumors and speculations of his time. Some, after all, believed the accused were really guilty, sometimes due to personal conviction, sometimes out of partisan prejudice, while others were certain that the confessions were a result of torture—either the torture of the accused or the threatened torture of their closest relatives.[7] Still others argued that the defendants were under hypnosis,[8] or ruled this out based on their courtroom behavior and instead pointed to the use of mescalin.[9] In Evreinov's play it is the character Nikolai Bukharin who asks: "No, really! What do they do in your dungeons to get people to confess to things they haven't even done?"[10]

Evreinov adds to the speculation in his play with a truth drug invented by the Secret police, "Veritophor," an "elixir of honesty" whose development is overseen by Yagoda. However, the drug is not used in the play for the defendants of the show trials, because the question is not how to extort the truth, but how to extort fiction. Yagoda uses the elixir for a private purpose, forcing a dose of it on Varvara, his mistress's sister, who is visiting Moscow from Paris, her home in exile. He does not want to find out what she really thinks about the Soviet Union—after all, he knows perfectly well the terrible

7   Examples of this appeared early on in Karlo Shteiner's autobiography and in Roy Medvedev's *Let History Judge*. Medvedev writes that the confessions were also extorted from Bukharin and Krestinsky, for example with the threat of murdering Bukharin's wife and newborn child. Roy A. Medvedev, *Let History Judge: The Origins and Consequences of Stalinism* (New York: Columbia University Press, 1989), 382.
8   See Erich Andermann, "Hexenprozess in Moskau?," *Das neue Tage-Buch* 6, February 1937, 162; S. Aberdam, "Hypnose in Moskau?," *Das neue Tage-Buch* 7, May 1937, 162–163.
9   See David Pike, *German Writers in Soviet Exile, 1933–1945* (Chapel Hill: University of North Carolina Press, 1962), 174.
10   Evreinov, *The Steps of Nemesis*, 32.

reality that he himself is helping to bring about—but he wants to hear whether Zinaida is "faithful" to him, whether she is not playing a trick on him. Evreinov has his characters reveal the political theater around them and develop methods for deciphering the acting of others, as Yagoda's confessions about his acting and the use of "Veritophor" suggest. In the time of the show trials, reality produced only theater and theatrical confessions. In Evreinov's play, on the other hand, it is the theater that produces the truth.

The Political Theatricalization of Life

It is no coincidence that Nikolai Evreinov, of all people, became interested in the Moscow show trials of the 1930s. Even though he studied the surviving accounts of the show trials, the protocols, and interviewed experts, one thing seemed to interest him above all: the inconceivable degree of theatricality that permeated politics in the Soviet Union. This meant not only the public staging, but above all the hidden theatricality, the theater that denied being theater. The show trials were the best example of the latter. They claimed to reveal the hidden truth of the opposition, and it was precisely this "hidden truth," which was to be proven with confessions and testimony, that was staged. The defendants were to confess as credibly as possible to crimes they had not committed.

Evreinov obviously recognized the theatricality of the show trials; his play brings them back onto the stage of the theater. At the same time, he saw that the call he had propagated in the 1910s for the "theatricalization of life" had been politically implemented in a completely different way, in a way that he probably had not anticipated. Was his play also an attempt to revise his own demand for the theatricalization of life?

In the 1910s, Evreinov's call for the theatricalization of life was directed primarily against the alleged 'naturalness' in theater and in life. "Theater without theatricality is rabbit stew without rabbits,"[11] Evreinov wrote in *Theater for Itself*, a three-volume book on the theater of the everyday that he wrote between 1915 and 1917. Behind this culinary comparison lay, above all, a polemic against Konstantin Stanislavsky's naturalistic school of acting. When Evreinov called for more theatricality then, he did not mean affected posturing. For Evreinov, theatricality was not limited to theater as an institution, but was an everyday practice and anthropological category.

With this broad concept of theater and theatricality, Evreinov's concept also differed from those of Stanislavsky's other contemporary opponents. Unlike, for example, Edward Gordon Craig, Vsevolod Meyerhold and Stanisław Witkiewicz, who also rejected Stanislavsky's naturalism, Evreinov saw no contradiction between the authentic or natural and the theatrical. Craig, Witkiewicz and Meyerhold, on the other hand, sought to overcome Stanislavsky's demand for naturalness and rejection of the mask primarily through a commitment to the total artificialization of the theater. Craig pursued this through the Übermarionette as a sublimated, depersonalized actor. Meyerhold's approach was 'biomechanics,' an anti-psychological, purely physiological training for actors, and Witkiewicz pushed for a 'pure,' metaphysical and artificial theater that should not be oriented towards life. Evreinov, on the other hand, claimed that theatricality was always

---

11   Nikolai N. Evreinov, *Demon teatral'nosti*, ed. by A. Ju. Zubkov and Vadim I. Maksimov (St. Petersburg: Letnij sad, 2002), 285.

already natural. In a way, he put an equal sign between naturalness and theater and added that precisely this so-called
naturalness was the most demanding element: "Oh, this
naturalness we know too well! This laughable naturalness,
outrageous in its naiveté! We have long since cracked it, and
Oscar Wilde even told us that this was the most difficult role
of all."[12]

In this respect, it is no wonder that Evreinov regarded
the Stalinist confession practice as a form of theater first and
foremost. It had degenerated into a mere ritual in the campaigns for "criticism and self-criticism" (*kritika i samokritika*)
as early as 1927. Just as Socialist Realism was not realism, the
ritualized confessions were not about truth. However, if someone articulated any real criticism, Stalin placed it in quotation
marks. He thus interpreted any criticism of his policies from
the outset as a false "criticism," which was only masquerad-
ing as criticism and was in reality sabotage and counterrevolutionary activity.[13] This inversion into opposites was Stalin's
political strategy: Facts were declared secret sabotage and lies
(disinformation) were staged as truth. For example, in 1936,
during the 1st Show Trial, *Pravda* published an article entitled
"On Enemies in Soviet Masks,"[14] while in March 1938, the
Deutsche Zentral-Zeitung (DZZ), the German-language organ
of the Communist Party published in Moscow, wrote of "Fascist murderers behind the masks of doctors,"[15] and then also
in March 1938, during the 3rd Trial, it was announced in the
newspaper *Bol'shevik* that Bukharin had worn the mask of

12   Ibid., 154.
13   Iosif V. Stalin, "Protiv oposhleniia lozunga samokritiki," *Sochineniia*,
vol. 11, 1928–mart 1929 (Moscow: Gos. izd-vo politicheskoi literatury, 1949),
127–136, here 133.
14   Hedeler, *Chronik der Moskauer Schauprozesse*, 58.
15   Ibid., 382.

a spy all his life.[16] In *Pravda*, Ezhov is praised for his ability to "recognize the enemy, no matter how he masks himself, and hold him accountable."[17] The metaphor of the mask was omnipresent, and the alleged unmasking served primarily to discredit critics in the ranks as fascists or fascist spies, not only in their own country but also internationally.

Evreinov, however, reverses the polarities once again and thus puts everything back in its place. In *Steps of Nemesis*, Evreinov uses theater not to unmask or expose the enemy, but to reveal theater through theater. It is crucial to note here that when he wrote of the "theatricalization of life," Evreinov did not mean to deceive and lie and to hide the theater, but to live out the natural instinct towards play, i.e. to show the theater as theater.

Therefore, in *Steps of Nemesis* Evreinov exposes the exposure itself as political theater. This is also made clear in one scene directly as a tip or stage direction from the designated head of the NKVD, Ezhov, to the prosecutor Andrei Vyshinsky, who directed the prosecution for the state during the show trials: "In your opening statement you need to emphasize as strongly as possible," Ezhov advises, "that all these Trotsky-ites, Zinovievites and Bukharinites are nothing but *capitulators*. That, concealing themselves with revolutionary phrases, they were seeking to re-establish capitalism in Russia."[18] Thus Evreinov verbally demonstrates how the mask that is to be torn off is created and put on in the first place by speech acts such as this.

---

16   Ibid., 395.
17   Ibid., 387.
18   Evreinov, *The Steps of Nemesis*, 132. Emphasis in the original.

The Theater Denied

So while the Soviet Union's judicial theater is based on hiding the staging at all costs and passing the truth off as a mask, Evreinov's theater is based on revealing the political theatricalization of life. It is perhaps surprising then that the Moscow show trials, which form such an important context for everything that happens in the play, are only shown in one scene. The remaining five scenes take place behind the scenes of power: in the apartment of Zinaida Popova, Yagoda's mistress and an invented distant relative of Bukharin; in Stalin's study in the Moscow suburb of Gorki; in a chemical laboratory of the Secret police at an unknown location, where the aforementioned "Veritophor" is produced and tested; in the office of the People's Commissar for Internal Affairs, Nikolai Ezhov, which is also a kind of dress rehearsal for the 3rd Trial, at least in the cross-examination of Bukharin; and finally in "hell," which is located in the room next to Ezhov's office during the dress rehearsal. In hell, the defendant Bukharin also confirms: "The trial between the authorities and the defendants doesn't take place in court, but behind the scenes; in Party committees, and not in the organs of the judicial investigation; in the Commissariat of Internal Affairs, and not in the Judiciary!"[19]

Bukharin, and thus Evreinov as well, does not assume that there is no theater behind the scenes. Rather, there is simply another theater off stage, and perhaps it is even the real one. Evreinov depicts this backstage theater as a kind of smear theater, a cabal of intrigues. Although many people tell the truth there, behind the scenes, they are just as likely to perform something for one another.

19   Ibid., 131.

The question is not so much whether they are acting, but how well and, above all, how credibly. In Evreinov's play, it is Stalin who is worried about the show trials' credibility: How could people "not be critical," he says, "when the accused exposed themselves in committing fairytale crimes and then even demanded the death penalty for them! It is completely absurd: no paper trail, no material evidence, not even a trace of any documents of any kind!" Stalin is not bothered by the theater itself, but by the "fairytale crimes," by the fantastic, amateurish presentation of evidence. When Yagoda asks Stalin how the production could be improved, whether he should have fabricated documents as well, Stalin has an idea: "Why *yourself*? What was needed was for the *criminals* to do it... Once a criminal admits to what we need, let him prepare a corresponding document to confirm it."[20]

Evreinov has Stalin formulate a solution to the problem that will enable him to dispose of his own staging. Or, in other words, a good staging is the one that one forces the others, one's political enemies, to produce on their own, in this case the defendants of the show trials.

Interestingly, in the historical show trials it was precisely the other way around. Prosecutor Andrei Vyshinsky had used the lack of evidence on the part of the prosecution as proof of guilt to justify the confession as the sole evidence. This was because Vyshinsky assumed that the offenses of which the defendants were accused would be primarily conspiratorial activity—if it had been executed in an appropriately professional manner, it would not have produced evidence of its existence at all. The more successful the conspiracy, the less evidence there would be, as Vyshinsky put it in his remarks to

20   Ibid., 41. Emphasis in the original.

the court: "How can one raise the question of evidence under these circumstances?"[21] The trick was more than ingenious, because in this way the prosecutor could always interpret the completely insufficient evidence as an indication of the crime. Vyshinsky concludes by reaffirming this claim: "I dare to assert, in accordance with the basic requirements of criminal procedural science, that in criminal cases for conspiracy one cannot make such claims."[22]

The Truth-Tellers

Evreinov's play not only presents the confession of the theater. It also tells us a great deal about Soviet reality. In doing so, Evreinov uses very different rhetorical tricks. He essentially turns the Stalinist principle of reversal into its opposite here as well. Those statements that are disqualified as brazen lies, paradoxically, are themselves particularly true. The truth thus emerges as a lie. Radek, for example, tells Stalin all kinds of unpleasant truths, but packages them as alleged statements of sabotage made by Tukhachevsky. Or Yagoda, who works himself into a fit: "The bastards! They accuse me of embezzlement, when I've saved the state *millions* with the free labor of prisoners! Enriched the Soviet Union with gigantic works that the Pharaohs of Egypt couldn't even dream of! Who made slave labor in the concentration camps so disciplined that we could supply it to state enterprises like a flawless product!"[23] And Ezhov is afraid that eventually people

21   Andrei J. Wyschinski, *Gerichtsreden* (Berlin: Dietz, 1951), 615.
22   Ibid., 615–616.
23   Evreinov, *The Steps of Nemesis*, 45. Emphasis in the original.

will say "he [Stalin] is settling personal scores with his former comrades."[24]

Evreinov allows himself a particularly interesting reversal in his portrayal of Bukharin. While the truth is passed off as a "lie" in the back rooms, the defendant Bukharin consistently tells the truth at the rehearsal for the trial, which also takes place in a back room: "Although I already have a poor opinion of our Soviet court, I confess that I would never in my life have believed that it would go so far as to accuse a man using *deliberately* falsified facts. I am completely disgusted and nauseous!"[25]

In the historical trial, this was not at all the case. It was precisely Bukharin's cross-examination that caused confusion. Bukharin, the party's chief ideologue and theoretician, had admitted almost everything he was accused of and even confessed to more than was necessary in his closing statement. Later it was learned that even during his imprisonment, before the beginning of the trials, he had written books, poems and philosophical arabesques and, on December 10, 1937, two months before the beginning of the 3rd Trial on March 2, 1938, he had written a letter of petition to Stalin. It is clear from the letter that at this point he still seemed to hope that Stalin would believe him and recognize his innocence. He even offers himself to Stalin as a Trotskyist detective and proposes he be given a 25-year sentence in Kolyma, which he could use to build a Siberian cultural center.[26] Why he wrote this and what it implied led to an international discussion that continues to this day. His appearance during the show

24   Ibid., 42.
25   Ibid., 124. Emphasis in the original.
26   Pis'mo N.I. Bukharina na imia I.V. Stalina, December 10, 1937, Russian State Archive of Socio-Political History (RGASPI), f.17, op. 171, d. 427, l. 12–22ob: http://istmat.info/node/62004.

trials was also repeatedly interpreted against the background of this letter. Why, people wondered, did he not disclose, as Nikolai Krestinsky had done, that he had been forced to confess to fabricated crimes?[27] Why did he humiliate himself in this way before Stalin and the entire nation?

Since then, there have been many interesting attempts to answer these questions, and Evreinov also participates in the speculation. Arthur Koestler, in *Darkness at Noon* (1940), was one of the first to deal with the intolerable situation of the accused who were required to slander themselves in order to justify the party line. Slavoj Žižek also reads the confessions of the accused in relation to this double role. In doing so, he draws attention to the Lacanian distinction between the subject of the statement (*sujet d'énoncé*) and the subject of the enunciation (*sujet d'énonciation*). In show trials, according to Žižek, the defendant, i.e. the victim, is required to admit to counterrevolution until he finally agrees with the judges' view that the death penalty is his just dessert, and thus paradoxically also "begins to like" his conviction:[28] "The accused finds himself in an absolute void insofar as he is compelled to authenticate his devotion to the communist cause by confessing his betrayal."[29] According to Žižek, the accused appear credible to the people only when

27   On Bukharin's strategy see also Medvedev, *Let History Judge*, 373; Klaus-Georg Riegel, *Konfessionsrituale im Marxismus-Leninismus* (Graz, Vienna and Cologne: Styria, 1985), 110–112; Sylvia Sasse, *Wortsünden. Beichen und Gestehen in der russischen Literatur* (Munich: Fink, 2009), 305–307; Karl Schlögel, *Terror und Traum. Moskau 1937* (Munich: Hanser, 2008), 665–667; Renate Lachmann, *Lager und Literatur. Zeugnisse des Gulag* (Konstanz. Konstanz University Press, 2019), 116–118.
28   Slavoj Žižek, *Grimassen des Realen. Jacques Lacan oder die Monstrosität des Aktes* (Cologne: Kiepenheuer und Witsch, 1991), 70–71.
29   Slavoj Žižek, *Liebe Dein Symptom wie Dich selbst* (Berlin: Merve, 1991), 53.

they accept the procedure of the show trials and assume their role in the staged drama, in order to return from this speech act to reality and to their role as a Communist who does not resist the Communist accusation. Bukharin, in his letter written before the trial, speaks of the "disarming" which was required of him: "I had no 'way out' but to confirm the accusations and testimonies of others and elaborate on them. Otherwise it would have seemed that I was 'not laying down my weapons'."[30]

But did Bukharin actually accept the role of traitor during the show trial, in the cross-examination with Vyshinsky and in his closing argument, did he actually "disarm" himself? Reading the published transcripts also makes another interpretation possible, because Bukharin's contradictory statements do not necessarily have to be read as a psychological dilemma. The censored protocols reveal that Bukharin actually split himself into two often contradictory subjects of speech, one subject of statement and one of testimony. Karl Schlögel writes that he confesses and recants at the same time.[31] But he does this on two different levels. Bukharin, for example, inquires of Vyshinsky before responding to the latter's questions, "You ask whether I, as a member of the centre of Rights and Trotskyites, was in favour … […] I was."[32] In other words, he inquires whether he was guilty in the role attributed to him or guilty as himself. Or elsewhere, "VYSHINSKY: Did you talk to Radek as the editor of "Izvestia" or as a member of the plotting organization? BUKHARIN: You understand perfectly well that I spoke to

---

30   Pis'mo N.I. Bukharina na imia I.V. Stalina.
31   Schlögel, *Terror und Traum*, 669.
32   *Report of Court Proceedings in the Case of the Anti-Soviet Bloc of Rights and Trotskyites* (Moscow, 1938), 377.

him as a member of the plotting organization..."[33] Bukharin distinguishes between speaking as Bukharin and speaking as the persona they invented for him during the cross-examination, as an alleged traitor, as if he were acting out a theatrical role. And it is only as this traitor that he confirms the accusations.

In his closing argument, moreover, Bukharin articulates the required split in terms of content; he speaks of a schizophrenia that accompanied his revolutionary actions. This schizophrenia, which is linked simultaneously to the crimes he is accused of and to the context of his testimony during the cross-examination, becomes clearest when he admits that he is guilty on all counts but denies the preconditions that enabled him to do this in the first place. Bukharin says that while he accepts responsibility for everything, that it was not his personal position. He pleads guilty even though he cannot remember specific acts, he admits to founding a gang without knowing the members of it, etc.[34] The closing argument ends with Bukharin admitting that he is guilty in his capacity as an accused counterrevolutionary criminal, but not as Bukharin. He splits himself into two speech subjects, not in order to "accept" his conviction, but to make the schizophrenic situation linguistically conceivable.

In Evreinov's case, however, Bukharin not only tells the truth, but also asks himself the question that became

33   Ibid., 405. This passage is missing in the Russian version. The English and German translations are much more comprehensive than the Russian 'original' published in 1938, in which sections are combined and where entire lines of argument are sometimes left out. Heinz Neumann and Margarete Buber-Neumann were commissioned to translate the text into German. Two months later Heinz Neumann was arrested. See Margarete Buber-Neumann, *Von Potsdam nach Moskau. Stationen eines Irrwegs* (Stuttgart: Ullstein Tachenbuchverlag, 1957), 439, 443.
34   See *Report of Court Proceedings*, 769.

a subject of so much discussion later, namely "To admit to vile, debased, disgusting acts! And even more, to do it almost ecstatically! I swear on my honor, I would rather be hanged, quartered and put to death under a dull saw!"[35] This is a Bukharin who is not yet in prison, who has not yet had to endure a public trial, this is the Bukharin who still has the opportunity to speak the truth even in public, a Bukharin as Evreinov might have wished him to be.

In his play, he does not have Bukharin shot three days after the verdict under Ezhov's supervision, but first sends him to the hell previously mentioned. There, Zinoviev advises him to confess: "My best advice: agree to any self-denunciation! Sign off on any crime! Agree to play the most humiliating role in the trial! As long as they *actually* shoot you, and not just on paper! Because [hell] is worse than death! A thousand times worse!"[36] Evreinov's contribution to the speculation over confessions is thus a fantastically dystopian one; surviving in Stalin's regime is worse than death, so it is better to confess to everything possible and more.

Theater as Punishment

Evreinov was no stranger to court trials or legal theory. He initially studied law between 1892 and 1901, but joined a theater group at law school, for which he wrote plays and performed. His thesis was in legal history and focused on the history of corporal punishment in Russia (*Istoriia telesnykh nakazaniakh v Rossii*). In it, he assembles material documenting public punishment in Russia since the Middle

---

35   Evreinov, *The Steps of Nemesis,* 29.
36   Ibid., 130.

Ages, referencing legal texts and listing types of punishment. It is not until 1912, in his collection of essays *Theater as Such* (*Teatr kak takovoi*), that he also explicitly reads the court of the 17th century Spanish Inquisition as theater, with its masked judges, torture props, and auto-da-fé. He is primarily concerned with commonalities between theater and court, theater and punishment, or, later, with common origins. Thus, in 1922, in "Theater and Scaffold" (*Teatr i Ėshafot*), he explores the coincidence of theater and court in the origins of tragedy, which, translated from Greek, is famously derived from the "goat song," and can be traced back to sacrificial rituals, public purifications, and self-abasement.[37] "Wherever we turn in search of the origin of the theater—whether to history, folklore, child psychology, or ethnography—everywhere we encounter visible or hidden signs of the scaffold, where the executioner and the victim (human or animal) in the early days of drama are the first to define the appeal of this new institution to the crowd, an institution that will only become theater later."[38]

After the October Revolution, when meetings were first held in the form of court trials, and finally agit courts began to play an increasingly important role in the public life of Soviet citizens as a moral-ideological compass, Evreinov had already emigrated to Paris. He does not seem to have come into contact with these parajuridical, amateur theatrical

---

37   Evreinov also reaches back to the roots of the theater in other studies and examines public purification (self-abasement) and the origins of tragedy, the "goat song" which was sung when a goat was sacrificed at the festival of Dionysus. Nikolai Evreinov, *Proiskhozhdenie dramy: folklor-icheskii ocherk. Pervobytnaia tragediia i rol' kozlu v istorii ee vozniknoveniia* (St. Petersburg: Petropolis, 1921).
38   Nikolai Evreinov, "Teatr i Ėshafot," in: *Segodnia*, June 6, 1996, 10 (First published in *Segodnia* 1922).

events. Yet he is responsible for one of the greatest political productions of the early Soviet Union as the director of *The Storming of the Winter Palace* (*Vziatie Zimnego dvortsa*), commissioned in 1920 for the 3rd anniversary of the October Revolution. Evreinov was hired as the principal director and bore enormous political responsibility. The importance of this event is reflected, among other things, in an order issued by the special commissioner of the fleet and army for the conduct of the October celebrations, the last paragraph of which, the 17th, announces that those who intend to disrupt the preparation and execution of the theatrical event will be accused of counterrevolutionary intent and brought before a revolutionary tribunal.[39]

It is likely that Evreinov saw in this commission, more than anything else, the potential for a gigantic production, something capable of eclipsing everything that had been done in the theater before it: the latest technology, 10,000 actors, 100,000 spectators. To what extent Evreinov understood that he had to realize a state commission to theatricalize history is not clear from his notes. The fact that one of the photos taken during the dress rehearsal for the theatrical storming was later used as a historical document would probably have amused him, since he believed theater has the potential to create reality and even to heal it. Evreinov, however, did not intend to falsify history. He always marked the spectacle as a spectacle.[40] His set consisted of two huge stages built on the

39   Nikolai Evreinov, "The Storming of the Winter Palace," in Nikolai Evreinov et al., *Storming of the Winter Palace*, ed. by Inke Arns, Igor Chubarov, and Sylvia Sasse (Berlin, Zurich: diaphanes, 2017), 30–49, here 45.
40   Igor' Chubarov, "'Teatralizatsiia zhizni' kak strategiia politizatsii iskusstva: Povtornoe vziatie Zimnego dvortsa pod rukovodstvom N.N. Evreinova (1920)," in Hans Günther and Sabine Hänsgen (eds.), *Sovetskaia vlast' i media* (St. Petersburg: Monoskop, 2005), 281–295.

square behind the Winter Palace, each 40 meters long. One of them showed the time before the October Revolution in the style of a comedy, almost as a parody of the past, while the other stage was supposed to show the revolution and the mobilization of the masses. In the history of the theater, the idea of the political mobilization of the masses matched the discovery of the spectator as an actor. Or, reversed and refor-mulated for the young Soviet Union: Discovering the specta-tor as an actor in the theater was an actualization of the politi-cal demand to mobilize the masses in the future dictatorship of the proletariat. Evreinov also used this historical moment to politicize his own concept of the theater. Before the dress rehearsal, he gave a speech in which he transferred aspects of his theory to the political situation: "The time of the extras is over. Remember, comrades, that you are not extras at all. You are artists. You are artists, possibly even more important art-ists than those of the old theater."[41]

By the 1930s, there was nothing left of this political enthusiasm. Political participation and the spontaneous activity of the masses were only representations that no lon-ger had a place in political reality; the political premises had themselves degenerated into ideological scenery. When Evre-inov was working on his article on "Theater and the Scaffold" in the early 1920s, his main concern was not to banish crime, vice, and punishment from the theater and not to turn the theater into a moral institution. Rather, he argued, Nemesis, the goddess of righteous retribution, should not be chased out of the theater, and should itself become the theater.[42] It is precisely in the theater, he argues, that there must be room for vice, crime, and punishment.

---

41 Evreinov, "Storming of the Winter Palace," 39–40.
42 Evreinov, "Teatr i Éshafot," 10.

Evreinov continued to write about the ideological objectives of early post-revolutionary theater in the 1930s. In an undated manuscript he delivered at a Parisian Masonic lodge after 1934, he writes that the performing arts in particular (theater, film, circus, festivals) had already been used to educate the masses immediately after the revolution.[43] Theater was particularly well suited to this purpose because it targeted consciousness as well as the emotions and the unconscious, and achieved its immediate effect through suggestion and direct involvement.

Evreinov does not recognize, however, that theater had become a punishment in the Soviet version of the theatricalization of life. This punitive function had already emerged in the agit courts, which were organized until about 1930. While the theater was still quite clearly marked in the agit courts until the mid-1920s, there, too, the dividing line became increasingly unclear. So it can happen that the village alcoholic is put on public display, has to play himself and to repent. This public repentance and confession, which was regularly rehearsed via the agit courts, culminated in the show trials, which completely concealed their theatricality. Michel Foucault stated in *Discipline and Punish* that one could observe how public punishment—a subject which had interested Evreinov since his dissertation for law school—gradually disappears and becomes discrete in modernity. Instead, the fear of punishment is transformed into the fear

---

43   Nikolai Evreinov, "Ideologiia sovetskogo teatra," Colombia University Libraries, Archival Collections, Rare Book & Manuscript Library, Nikolai Nikolaevich Evreinov Papers, ca. 1905–1965, Box 12, 34. Lectures that he delivered through his membership to the Free Masons were published in Nikolai N. Evreinov, *Tainye pruzhiny iskusstva. Stat'i po filosofii iskusstva, ėtike i kul'turologii (1920–1950)*, ed. by Igor' Chubarov (Moscow: Logos-Al'tera, 2004).

of confession. This is also partly true for the political show trials. In the show trials, we can also observe a discrepancy in punishment that occurs on the level of staging; while the executions do not take place in public, the confession is put on display.[44] It is true that the show trials are—on the surface—staged as cathartic theater, as the epitome of a moral institution that reveals how conspiracy, murder, crime and espionage have been successfully uncovered and thwarted. On the other hand, the show trial is itself the crime. The purification is en*acted*, and is first produced by a "theatrical pact" with the accused. When this happens, the theater itself becomes the punishment. The "theatrical pact," however, occurs not only on the level of political staging; it also reenacts itself in everyday life. Everywhere people "play along." Fellow travelers should actually be called fellow players. Nor is it only the fellow travelers who play along: To do so becomes a daily struggle for existence. The "theatrical pact" demanded by the dictatorship is perhaps the most common everyday political theater.

Evreinov, however, seems much more concerned with another question, the role of the spectators. The fact that he makes Nemesis the title figure of his play also reflects the role of the spectators or fellow players: Varvara sees the Russian people as potential enactors of the role of Nemesis: "The Russian people suffer patiently, but when their hour of revenge comes the whole world will shake from their wrath. You just wait—they will repay you a hundredfold for the millions of people you've martyred, killed, tortured, humiliated, and who took their own lives in despair!"[45] Seeing the people once

---

44   See Michel Foucault, *Discipline and Punish: The Birth of the Prison* (New York: Pantheon Books 1977), 93ff.
45   Evreinov, *The Steps of Nemesis,* 75.

more in the role of actors, and not as mere extras and or spectators, is perhaps the utopic vision hidden in the play. When Yagoda, however, deposed as head of the secret service, turns to the audience at the end and justifies himself: "Well, you might as well ham it up if the people will put up with a travesty!,"[46] then the statement becomes all the more agonizing and remains relevant today. Why do we allow political theater to play itself out for us?

46   Ibid, 139.

Gleb J. Albert

Evreinov's Archive
Imagining the Moscow Show Trials in Exile

1. "What is going on in the USSR?"

When Herbert Wehner, at the time a KPD (Communist Party of Germany) functionary in Moscow's Comintern headquarters who would later become an influential early SPD politician in West Germany, compiled secret morale reports from KPD cells operating in the German underground in March 1938, the Moscow show trials were a dominant theme. "What is going on in the USSR? Why these convictions? There is a great controversy about it among our colleagues," read the report of a Berlin KPD cell.[1] The proceedings in Moscow were not only a subject of controversy but also a central source of uncertainty and doubt. "These trials," it is said elsewhere, "are very repulsive"; the workers "don't believe everything that is said about them."[2] At the party base, the show trials were even "seen as symptoms of degeneration, even by workers identified as anti-fascists."[3]

It was not only the Communist resisters in Nazi Germany who were deeply unsettled by the news from Moscow. When leading Bolsheviks, heroes of the October Revolution and

1   Hermann Weber et al., eds., *Deutschland, Russland, Komintern, Bd. 2: Dokumente (1918–1943). Nach der Archivrevolution: Neuerschlossene Quellen zu der Geschichte der KPD und den deutsch-russischen Beziehungen,* Archive des Kommunismus – Pfade des XX. Jahrhunderts 6 (Berlin: De Gruyter, 2015), 1429.
2   Ibid., 1424.
3   Ibid., 1426.

those who had been leaders early on in the party were put on trial and accused of the most monstrous crimes in August 1936, no one abroad could explain what was going on in Stalin's Soviet Union. In January 1937 and then finally in March 1938, when two more show trials brought charges against numerous revolutionaries, functionaries, scholars and military officers, who were tried and mostly shot, the confusion only persisted.

The Moscow Trials occupied all political, cultural, and social groups that had even the slightest connection with the Soviet Union or communism. These topics were far from being irrelevant at that time. The "Popular Front" strategy proclaimed by the Comintern from 1935 on seemed to herald a kind of thaw between Communists and democratic anti-fascists; the Communist-backed Front Populaire government in France and the Frente Popular in Spain, with the participation of the Spanish CP, were only the most visible political manifestations of this new approach. Wide circles of Western intellectuals saw Stalin's regime, notwithstanding all the crimes it was already known to have committed, as a tangible and determined ally against European fascism in Germany, Spain, Italy, and elsewhere. This image was seriously marred by the spectacle of the Soviet Union inflicting such harm to itself at a critical moment in European history by sending prominent politicians and military officers to the scaffold. But for the time being, many prominent anti-fascist intellectuals preferred to trust the official Soviet statements and not to be dissuaded from believing in the "anti-fascist myth" of the Soviet Union. Only the Stalin-Hitler Pact, concluded in August 1939, would finally cause real damage to the myth.[4] Until then, however,

4   Bernhard H. Bayerlein, "Abschied von einem Mythos. Die UdSSR, die Komintern und der Antifaschismus 1930–1941," *Osteuropa* 59, no. 7–8

luminaries of anti-fascist literature such as Heinrich Mann insisted that everything was above board at the trials.[5] Even Lion Feuchtwanger, invited by the regime to attend the 2nd Moscow Trial as an observer, struggled with great doubts and inner conflict, but ultimately came out in favor of Moscow's "truth."[6]

While "fellow travelers" in the Popular Front period found it difficult to understand what was happening behind the scenes in Moscow, other groups that had a closer relationship to the Soviet Union harbored far fewer illusions. First and foremost were the followers of Leon Trotsky, the revolutionary, theoretician, and former leading Bolshevik exiled by Stalin in 1927. Trotskyists had an especially strong motivation to defend their honor. This is because, in the show trials, Trotsky was made into the chief defendant in absentia and the embodiment of absolute evil. In addition, Trotsky and other members of the Left Opposition had already presented detailed critical analyses of the Stalin regime in the early 1930s and had brought the term "Stalinism" into circulation in the first place.[7] Trotsky threw himself into the journalistic battle against the Moscow Trials. His son Leon Sedov had published

(2009): 125–148; Bernhard H. Bayerlein, *"Der Verräter, Stalin, bist Du!". Vom Ende der linken Solidarität. Komintern und kommunistische Parteien im Zweiten Weltkrieg 1939–1941. Mit einem Beitrag von Wolfgang Leonhard. Unter Mitarbeit von Natal'ja S. Lebedeva, Michail Narinskij und Gleb Albert* (Berlin: Aufbau-Verlag, 2008).

5   Julijana Ranc, "Franz Pfemfert gegen Heinrich Mann. Dokumente und Argumente zu einer vergessenen Kontroverse," *Exil* 22, Nr. 2 (2004): 18–35.

6   Anne Hartmann, *"Ich kam, ich sah, ich werde schreiben". Lion Feuchtwanger in Moskau 1937. Eine Dokumentation*, Akte Exil, Neue Folge 1 (Göttingen: Wallstein Verlag, 2017); Lion Feuchtwanger, *Moskau 1937. Ein Reisebericht für meine Freunde* (Berlin: Aufbau Taschenbuch, 1993).

7   Christoph Jünke, ed., *Marxistische Stalinismuskritik im 20. Jahrhundert. Eine Anthologie* (Cologne: ISP, 2017).

The Red Book: On the Moscow Trial in 1936, where he fundamentally deconstructed the accusations of Stalin's prosecutors in the first Moscow Trial.[8] He was most likely murdered by the NKVD while in exile in Paris in 1938 for his political activities.

But even beyond the Trotskyist groups, it was primarily leftists, often former Communists, who were the first to set out in search of answers to the disturbing events in Moscow. This is not surprising; after all, they had dedicated their lives to the revolution and had initially cultivated an unconditional loyalty to the state that emerged from that revolution. It is no coincidence that the first literary treatments of the show trials came from precisely those circles. Probably the best known of these is the novel *Darkness at Noon*, written immediately after the trials in 1939 by Arthur Koestler, a former KPD and Comintern journalist who became a "renegade" in reaction to Stalin's terror. The novel presents the reflections of an imprisoned former revolutionary and his decision to take on the most outrageous charges in favor of the "cause."[9] Victor Serge, revolutionary writer and former member of Trotsky's Left Opposition, also wrote his *Midnight in the Century* between 1936 and 1938, under the immediate impression of the show trials, where he traced the path from the targeted persecution of oppositionists in the 1920s and early 1930s to the indiscriminate mass terror of the late 1930s by literary means.[10]

8   Leon Sedov, *The Red Book: On the Moscow Trial* (London: New Park Publications, 1980).

9   Horst Möller, "Arthur Koestler: Sonnenfinsternis," in *Deutsch-russische Kulturbeziehungen im 20. Jahrhundert. Einflüsse und Wechsel-wirkungen*, ed. by Horst Möller and Aleksandr O. Čubar'jan (Berlin: De Gruyter Oldenbourg, 2016), 107–115.

10   Susan Weissman, *Victor Serge: A Political Biography* (London: Verso, 2013), 197–198; Victor Serge, *Midnight in the Century*, translated by Richard Greeman (London: Writers and Readers, 1982).

In addition to the radical left, whose relationship to the "fatherland of the working people" was abruptly called into question by the show trials, there was another group whose self-image and debates were closely tied to Russia: counter-revolutionary and anti-Bolshevik émigrés who had already gone abroad during the revolutionary and civil war periods. Naturally, they had a different view of the show trials than the Left Oppositionists. They had never harbored illusions about the Bolsheviks, and accordingly watched the internecine retributions with satisfaction. In the émigré press, there was even a certain schadenfreude over the trials and the executions of the old revolutionary guard. The liberal *Novoe Slovo* in Paris, for example, wrote in January 1937 in response to Karl Radek's conviction: "We fully share the characterization made by the Soviet press regarding Radek. [...] We wrote the same about Radek 15 years ago."[11] A certain segment of those in political exile was even thoroughly Stalinophile and sympathetic to the Soviet dictator by the early 1930s, as he settled scores with the leading internationalist Bolsheviks and nurtured hopes for the rebirth of Russia as a strong state. This attitude persisted in sections of the exile press through the first two Moscow Trials, when some émigré newspapers replicated Soviet pronouncements on the trials without comment. Only the trial of Tukhachevsky and other military leaders in June 1937 led to a reevaluation in these circles.[12] But whether one dismissed the Moscow Trials as an internal reckoning or even welcomed them, there were few reflections on the character of the trials *qua* show trials or, beyond that,

11   As cited in Julitta Suomela, *Zarubezhnaia Rossiia: Ideino-politicheskie vzgliady russkoi emigratsii na stranitsakh russkoi evropeiskoi pressy v 1918–1940 gg.* (St. Petersburg: Kolo, 2004), 269.
12   Ibid., 215–227, 267–271.

on Stalinist society generally, in Russian emigration outside of left circles.

Nikolai Evreinov's *The Steps of Nemesis* therefore stands out all the more as a lucid artistic reflection on the show trials and Stalin's terror, especially when one considers that Evreinov cannot be ascribed to any of the aforementioned groups. Even though he staged mass theater on behalf of the Bolsheviks in the early 1920s, he was not a convinced Communist. And even if *The Steps of Nemesis*, like almost all publications from the anti-Bolshevik emigration, used the pre-revolutionary orthography, he did not belong to "White" Russia either in terms of worldview or milieu. Evreinov was a classic "*nevozvrashchenets*," a "non-returnee." Like thousands of other cultural workers, scientists, and even party functionaries and state officials, he had decided not to return to Russia from an authorized trip abroad in early 1925. The "non-returnees" were ideologically a highly heterogeneous group. Abroad, their insider knowledge enabled them to become sought-after experts, but at the same time they were often eyed suspiciously by the "old" emigration and subjected to the blanket suspicion of being opportunists and turncoats.[13]

Sylvia Sasse writes in detail in this volume about *The Steps of Nemesis* as Evreinov's reaction as a theorist of the "theatricalization of life" to the macabre theater of Stalinist mock justice. In doing so, she emphasizes that Evreinov did not intend to create a work of historically verified documentary theater with *Nemesis*. And, correspondingly, my task as a historian here is not to point out the discrepancies between Evreinov's reconstruction of events and the history of the

13   Vladimir Genis, *Nevernye slugi rezhima. Pervye sovetskie nevozvrashchentsy, 1920–1933. Opyt dokumental'nogo issledovaniia. 2 vols.* (Moscow: s.n., 2009–2012).

show trials. That would not only be pedantic, but would also be trivial. It would not do justice to the horizon of the historical protagonists. Instead, my focus here will be on the "memory" of the text, which, according to Renate Lachmann, lies in the "intertextuality of its references."[14] In other words, what follows is an attempt to reconstruct Evreinov's archive, the material arsenal he relied on while working on the play, and at the same time to interrogate the text itself as an archive of emigré knowledge of the show trials and Stalinism.[15] As his widow Anna Kashina-Evreinova points out in the preface to the play, Evreinov, almost obsessively, gathered all the information he thought might be useful for understanding the incomprehensible events in the homeland. Which voices and perspectives on the Soviet Union and Stalin's terror served as material for Evreinov's play, and which, in turn, were left out? What does this mean for the way Evreinov makes sense of the show trials and thus, more broadly, of Stalinist society?

2. Evreinov's Archive

When trying to trace the material Evreinov used, a vast panorama comes into view. Anna Kashina-Evreinova's characterization of Evreinov's research as an almost "deranged

14   Renate Lachmann, *Gedächtnis und Literatur. Intertextualität in der russischen Moderne* (Frankfurt am Main: Suhrkamp, 1990), 36.
15   The Evreinov *fond* at the Russian State Archive of Literature and Art (RGALI) in Moscow actually contains individual items Evreinov collected on the Moscow Trials, as part of his collection of materials on theater and justice (fond 982, opis' 1, delo 302). See V. V Ivanov, ed., *Mnemozina. Dokumenty i fakty iz istorii russkogo teatra XX veka*, vol. 1 (Moscow: Indrik, 1996), 19. Due to the global pandemic, this *fond* was not accessible to the author, but it can be assumed that it represents only a small part of the materials that make up the "archive" of *The Steps of Nemesis*.

obsession" does not seem far from the truth, even if we leave out the pathological emphasis. The author draws on an impressive fund of knowledge about the Soviet Union from the Revolutionary and Civil War periods through the 1930s, relying on a volume of information far beyond the average knowledge horizon of Russian emigrés.

First, Evreinov's commanding overview of official Soviet pronouncements from the time of the show trials is striking. He draws on the full range of stenographic reports of the trials published almost immediately after the respective trials—and, as we know now, heavily abridged and distorted by the censors.[16] The sixth scene, the key scene of the play, where the new NKVD chief Ezhov holds a macabre dress rehearsal of the court theater together with prosecutor Vyshinsky, is largely based on the transcript of the 3rd Moscow Trial, whose set pieces Evreinov weaves into the dramaturgy he imagines of this event, which has neither been handed down nor recorded. Evreinov also followed the reporting of the Soviet press very closely. The smallest details of the coverage (which was not merely reporting, but helped determine the course of the show trials) find their way into *Nemesis,* such as a newspaper note in the aftermath of the 1st Moscow Trial that nominally cleared Bukharin of suspicion of co-conspiracy, but was actually published with the conscious intent of giving Bukharin, who would later become the primary defendant in the 3rd Moscow Trial, a false sense of security. Evreinov similarly drew on an inconspicuous news item that demoted the

16   On the publication history see Wladislaw Hedeler, "Ezhov's Scenario for the Great Terror and the Falsified Record of the Third Moscow Show Trial," in *Stalin's Terror: High Politics and Mass Repression in the Soviet Union*, ed. by Barry McLoughlin and Kevin McDermott (Basingstoke: Palgrave Macmillan, 2004), 34–55.

all-powerful GPU chief Genrikh Yagoda to chief postmaster, clearing the way for his ouster and arrest.

However, the Soviet mass media served Evreinov not only as a source of factual information, but also as an inspiration. They allowed him to recreate the hysterical and highly paranoid discourse of high Stalinism—for example in the longer passages from Soviet radio speeches that appear several times in the play. Although it cannot be determined precisely whether these are faithful reproductions of authentic radio material or whether Evreinov invented these passages himself, inspired by the Stalinist discourse about the "enemies of the people," certain nuances of the passages at least suggest the latter interpretation, as they deviate too strongly from the conventional repertoire of Stalinist propaganda. If this is indeed true, Evreinov once again takes the hysterical discourse of high Stalinism to the extreme. For example, by his inclusion of the sentence about the vengeful goddess Nemesis into the radio speech in the fifth scene, with the radio speaker claiming she has no more patience with the enemies of the Soviet Union, and then closing the broadcast with an almost surreal poem, supposedly from the pen of a "Soviet bard". In doing so, Evreinov plays a game with the expectations of readers and viewers, a game which has lost nothing in its effect due to our distance from the historical events—quite the opposite. Today's reader, even an historian, cannot be one hundred percent sure: Was Stalinist propaganda really so phantasmagorical? Or is Evreinov satirizing it by making it seem even more phantasmagorical than it already was?

The author was also well informed about the official popular culture of high Stalinism, albeit from the safe distance of exile. The latest Soviet pop songs are used to accompany the play's ceremonial scenes; the heroes recite the odes of the Soviet Kazakh folk bard and Stalin admirer Dzhambul, as well as topical verses by the Kremlin court poet Demian Bedny. Evreinov also makes extensive use of a particularly perfidious example of Stalinist cultural production and policy, the "lavishly produced illustrated volume" that Zinaida pulls off the shelf in the first scene to convince her skeptical sister of the merits of the Soviet system. This is the luxuriously illustrated book on the construction of the Belomor Canal, published in 1934. Under the oversight of Maxim Gorky, an entire brigade of Soviet cultural figures (including such famous names as Viktor Shklovsky, Mikhail Zoshchenko, Alexei Tolstoy, Vera Inber, Valentin Kataev, and Bruno Jasieński) had produced this book to put a humanist gloss on slave labor in the GULag.

Evreinov's trove of material, however, includes not only the contemporary products of Stalinism, but also a large body of knowledge and material from the Civil War and NEP years. Much of it may be things that he had perceived and "stored away" when he himself was still in Soviet Russia: for example, Radek's call in mid-1918 to have enemies of the revolution publicly shot. Similarly, Bukharin's quotations on the violence of the proletarian dictatorship, which are turned against the defendant by the prosecutors in Evreinov's imagined "dress rehearsal" for the trial (but not in the historical trial itself), do not come from his well-known party textbook, the *ABC of Communism*, but from a half-forgotten 1918 precursor text, the *Program of the Communists*. In addition, Evreinov draws on a wide range of memoir literature to better characterize his protagonists. These include the memoirs of the imaginist Anatoly Mariengof, used as the basis for Bukharin's description, or the memoirs of the former Bolshevik Vladimir Voitinsky, the origin of the unflattering statements by Lenin. Even the Swiss Communist Fritz Platten's 1924 vindication pamphlet, *Die Reise Lenins durch Deutschland im plombierten Wagen*, is used, with Radek's character mentioning it to Stalin to emphasize his own contribution to Lenin's return from Swiss exile.

A further and central component of Evreinov's fund of material is the exile press. He not only took Soviet propaganda material from it, such as the poem in praise of Yagoda by young prisoners, which he had apparently read in a feature article by the exiled former prime minister of the Provisional Government, Alexander Kerensky.[17] Evreinov also drew inspiration for entire plot lines from Soviet reporting in the exile press, such as in Scene Four, where he has Yagoda quote passages from the play *The Shot* by the Komsomol poet Alexander Bezymensky, reading it through an interpretation critical of Stalin. The play, which premiered in 1929, was a scandal at the time, not least because it included a direct attack on Mikhail Bulgakov. However, Bezymensky was a Trotsky supporter in 1923 but a loyal Stalinist by the time of the play in 1929.[18] The interpretation of the play as a critique of Stalin was made explicit primarily by the exile press, which cited precisely those passages that Evreinov quotes in *The Steps of Nemesis*.[19] Beyond the exile press, memoirs and exposés by Russian émigrés were another important component of Evreinov's sources of inspiration and information. As will be seen below, this conditioned the author's particular view of the dynamics of rule in high Stalinism.

---

17   See A. Kerenskii, "Golos izdaleka," *Novaia Rossiia*, 11 April 1937.
18   On Bezymensky and his political shift see Aleksandr V. Reznik, *Trotskii I tovarishchi. Levaia oppozitsiia I politicheskaia kul'tura RKP(b) 1923–1924* (St. Peterburg: Izdatel'stvo EUSPb, 2017), 139–140.
19   See *Vozrozhdenie*, August 18, 1929.

3. Intrigues in the Court of the Red Tsar

The history of Stalin's regime as a story of intrigues and machinations at the command heights of power was the preferred narrative in writing about Stalinism for a long time, beginning with the first period of émigré memoirs and journalism and continuing in political science and historical scholarship through the Cold War. Even today it still reappears occasionally, as when, for example, the British historian Simon Sebag Montefiore titles his book on the power intrigues under Stalin *The Court of the Red Tsar*.[20] Meanwhile, in social history and, most recently, with the "revisionism debate" in the 1980s, a broader view of the social causes and dynamics of Stalinism has been uncovered.[21] Looking at the personal relationships at the top of power remains productive and legitimate, however, for without the friendship and patronage networks and the dependency relationships linked to them, which Stalin actively expanded and used in his capacity as general secretary of the party from 1922 onward in order to oust his opponents in the party, the power dynamics of Stalinism at the time of the show trials cannot be understood either.[22] But interwar émigrés also had another reason for preferring to write about intrigues and internal party disputes among the Communists and less (and

20   Simon Sebag Montefiore, *Stalin: The Court of the Red Tsar* (New York: Knopf, 2004).

21   On the "revisionism debate" in the history of the Soviet Union see most recently Ronald Grigor Suny, *Red Flag Unfurled: History, Historians, and the Russian Revolution* (London: Verso, 2017).

22   Gerald M. Easter, *Reconstructing the State. Personal Networks and Elite Identity in Soviet Russia* (Cambridge: Cambridge University Press, 2000); Reznik, *Trotskii i tovarishchi*; Sheila Fitzpatrick, *On Stalin's Team. The Years of Living Dangerously in Soviet Politics* (Princeton: Princeton University Press, 2015).

especially less concretely) about what was happening among the broader masses of the Soviet population. In their eyes, the October Revolution (and, depending on their political outlook, even the February Revolution) was the result of a conspiracy and a coup and had no social basis. Thus, the only decisive factor for Russia's fate was the question of personal power: if it could fall, Bolshevism would fall, and then Russia would be free.

Evreinov also chooses to look at the intrigues of the powerful in *Nemesis*. This owes to the fact that one of his central sources of information is the 1930 tell-all book by Boris Bazhanov, another prominent "non-returnee," whose name Evreinov explicitly mentions several times. Born in 1900, Bazhanov joined the Communist Party as a student and served as an aide in Stalin's secretariat from 1923 to 1925. In 1928, disillusioned with Communism, he organized an official visit to Central Asia under false pretenses and spectacularly fled from there to the West via Persia and India. He settled in Paris and, after a few articles in the émigré press, published the book *I Was Stalin's Secretary*, which appeared in French and German, but not in Russian or English. A Russian edition, fundamentally revised by the author, was only published in 1980, long after Evreinov's death.[23] The latter may have read the French or German editions of the book, or perhaps Russian-language preprints or other articles by Bazhanov in the émigré press, since some of the quotations he cites do not correspond to the published editions of the book.

---

23 Boris Bazhanov, *Vospominaniia byvshego sekretaria Stalina* (s.l.: Tret'ia volna, 1980). English edition: Boris Bazhanov, *Bazhanov and the Damnation of Stalin*, translated by David W. Doyle (Athens: Ohio University Press, 1990).

Bazhanov's book is person-centered to the extreme; the "common people" do not appear in his work, except in the role of extras or as metaphors. Instead, he provides dozens of character studies of the leading Bolsheviks as well as the subalterns in Stalin's entourage, including character details that were demonstrably untrue, such as the claim that Alexander Rykov was a severe alcoholic—a detail that Evreinov reuses prominently in the play. In keeping with this person-centeredness, Bazhanov's account is permeated with the notion that the course of history is in the hands of individuals. He makes himself into the chief exponent of this outlook when he emphasizes at various points that *he* prepared, influenced, or averted this or that decision by Stalin or other leaders. Even though Evreinov draws excessively from Bazhanov's collection of rumors, situational sketches and character portraits, he very clearly does not take up this view of history as decided by individuals. We see this in Ezhov's bloody power struggle in the NKVD to oust Yagoda. It constitutes one of the central plot points of *Nemesis*, and gestures instead towards the idea that powerful persons in high Stalinism are actually interchangeable, as long as they are subservient to "Uncle Joe."

One aspect that marks Evreinov's play as clearly influenced by Bazhanov is the continuing presence of intrigue, factionalism, and conspiracy. Although the reliability of Bazhanov's account is questionable at many points, it does fairly accurately portray the atmosphere of the period he describes. The years between 1923 and 1926 were marked by bitter fights between supporters of different party factions, fought both behind the scenes and in public. These events not only fascinated the early Soviet public; they were also followed by anti-Bolsheviks in exile and were publicized almost gleefully, as evidenced by numerous commentaries and caricatures in the émigré press.[24]

It is highly debatable what role such intrigues and faction-building played from the mid-1930s, in the run-up to the show trials and the Great Terror. The monstrous conspiracy charges against the defendants were all fabricated—this much is evident—and today it is only Stalinist pseudo-scholars who question this fact, especially in Russia. What is certainly undisputed is that most of the prominent defendants had really opposed Stalin politically at certain times. Thus Stalin was able to mix fragments of real oppositional history with phantasmagorical conspiracy constructs, as in the case of the accusations against Bukharin in the 3rd Moscow Trial, which Evreinov used extensively, when the former chief theoretician of the party is confronted over his real opposition to Lenin in 1918, but this is linked to completely fictitious plans to assassinate Lenin and Stalin. Trotsky had already described such constructs on the occasion of the Kirov murder in 1934 and again and again in the course of the Moscow Trials as an "amalgam," i.e. as an artificial fusion of materials of different quality.[25]

It is plausible that oppositional Bolsheviks had not necessarily changed their convictions even under high Stalinism. Nor can it be ruled out that they might have clandestinely criticized Stalin among themselves.[26] However, we

24   Suomela, *Zarubezhnaia Rossiia,* 199–202.
25   Leon Trotsky, *On the Kirov Assassination* [1934], translated by John G. Wright (New York: Pioneer Publishers, 1956).
26   Such is the direction taken by the anti-Stalinist Russian historian Aleksandr Shubin, who points to the oppositional past and pre-revolutionary underground experience of the protagonists of the show trials. In this, he at least does not rule out the possibility of conspiracies among them, although of course not in the form in which they were accused by the prosecutors. Aleksandr V. Shubin, *Vozhdi i zagovorshchiki. Politicheskaia bor'ba v SSSR v 1920-1930-kh godakh* (Moscow: Veche, 2004).

can safely say it is impossible that their oppositional meetings could have taken place as Evreinov imagines them, with heretical speeches in the salon and guests singing anti-Stalin songs at a family party. The claustrophobic atmosphere on the eve of the Great Terror, where everyone distrusted everyone, especially among the (former) party elite, would never have allowed Bukharin, Rykov, Radek, and others to expose themselves so publicly. However, it would be pointless and misguided to blame Evreinov for his—in hindsight—ahistorical imagination. Rather, the way he stages the informal politics of the 1930s shows us how much he sees the Soviet Union of the 1930s through the lens of the 1920s, conditioned on the one hand by his own experiences, and on the other by his choice of sources.

4. The 1920s as a Model

The extent to which Evreinov's Moscow of the 1930s is shaped by his view of the 1920s is evident at numerous points. For example, his decision to place the ritual of an "Octobering" (*oktiabriny*) at the center of the plot. The ceremony was part of the "new life" envisioned by the Bolsheviks and was designed as a replacement for the traditional baptism of the church. It caused quite a stir, even though it ultimately failed to establish itself.[27] Evreinov would have taken great interest in such a theatricalized ritual. The close resemblance between the October baptism sequence in the play and the models for October baptisms circulated by early Soviet agitprop is itself

---

27   Elena V. Dianova, "Evoliutsiia praktiki imianarecheniia v pervye desiatiletiia sovetskoi vlasti," *Istoriia povsednevnosti*, no. 1 (2021): 76–103.

good evidence of his outsized interest in the phenomenon.[28] But "Octoberings," which were already more a matter of propaganda than a part of everyday life in the 1920s, had almost completely disappeared by the 1930s. The cultural restoration which took place under Stalin no longer had any place for radical rituals of the "new life."

Even in terms of the regime's repression of the general population, Evreinov's play still largely reflects the conditions of the 1920s and early 1930s. The protagonists continue to speak of the "concentration camps," the common name for the Soviet regime's penal camps in the 1920s, and Solovki and Narym appear as places of imprisonment, places that were already notorious as places of exile during the tsarist era and whose horrors took place and became public knowledge primarily in the 1920s. At its most contemporary, characters mention the construction of the Belomor Canal by camp prisoners and the great famine of the early 1930s. Absent, however, are the mass terror and the accompanying massive social paranoia of the second half of the 1930s. The character of the nanny, who is released from the "concentration camp" on the eve of the Great Terror to work for the mistress of one of the top state functionaries, is particularly anachronistic.

Seemingly incidental details—details, however, which will catch the eye of those familiar with the history of the early Soviet Union—bring into sharp relief how the 1920s, rather than the 1930s, are the main material used to tell the (pre) story of Stalin's terror. When Yagoda forcibly administers a truth serum to the Parisian émigré Varvara, he is interrupted

28   See O. M. Beliaeva, "'Krasnaia' obriadnost' kak instrument politicheskogo vospitaniia sovetskikh grazhdan," *Arkhivy Sankt-Peterburga* (blog), no year, https://spbarchives.ru/cgaipd_publications/-/asset_publisher/yV5V/content/id/668135.

by a call from a colleague in the secret police and has to give him torture tips. The man on the other end of the line is identified as Osip Brik, a prominent figure in the 1920s literary scene. Brik, a member of the early Soviet avant-garde and an important theorist of formalism, was a scandalous figure not only because his wife, Lilia Brik, had an open love affair with Vladimir Mayakovsky, *the* early Soviet model poet, but also because he worked for a time in the Petrograd Cheka. He did not, however, do so as an informer or torturer, but as a trained lawyer. He was employed in the legal department of the secret police and was dismissed as an "element alien to the class" as early as 1923. Even if it cannot be ruled out that Evreinov had a personal score to settle with Brik and therefore inserted him in the play as a bloody torturer, in reality Brik had long since ceased to be part of the secret police apparatus by the time of the Great Terror, and, moreover, Brik's notoriety as a scandalous figure had also long since fizzled out by then and was hardly capable of exciting anyone's imagination, except perhaps those who vividly remembered the cultural life of the 1920s.

Even Brik's torture victim, an archbishop and "Tikhonite," is a relic of the early 1920s. The struggle that took place from 1922 to 1924 within the Russian Orthodox Church between the followers of Tikhon and the "Renovationists" (*obnovlentsy*), supported and at the same time instrumentalized by the Bolsheviks, had long since been played out by the mid-1930s. By the beginning of the decade, the disputes between the "Tikhonites" and the "Renovationists" were a non-issue; clergymen of both tendencies were persecuted equally, and the "Renovationists" were persecuted even more intensely by the middle of the 1930s.[29] The Tikhonite movement, on

29   Grigorii Babaian, "Obnovlenchestvo v gody repressii i Velikoi Otechestvennoi Voiny," August 11, 2017, https://sdamp.ru/news/n5168/

the other hand, was rehabilitated after Germany's attack on
the Soviet Union and incorporated into the state apparatus.
Again, the point is not to reproach Evreinov for not having
been up to date in matters of Soviet religious policy. Rather,
the episode testifies to the difficulties that even someone
who came from Russia and had lived under the Bolsheviks for
several years faced when looking at the Stalinist Soviet Union
from the outside.

5. A Parable of Stalinism?

Given how Evreinov brings high Stalinism to the stage using
the scenery of the 1920s, as it were, his play does not seem
interested in Stalinism as a social phenomenon and does not
offer any corresponding attempts at interpretation, at least
at first glance. We learn about repressions of the Soviet state
as they were already practiced in the first decade after 1917,
while the specifics of Stalinist mass terror are largely absent.
We are offered political conspiracies and intrigues that could
have taken place in other authoritarian and totalitarian so-
cieties. *Nemesis* is free of the claustrophobic atmosphere of
high Stalinism, when everyone had to be on guard against everyone else, an atmosphere that Osip Mandelstam captured
in 1933 in his famous Stalin epigram, "We live, without feeling the country beneath,/Ten paces away no one hears that
we speak". The systematic analyses of Stalinism that were
already emerging at the time the play was written—and especially from the left, on the part of communist dissidents and
oppositionists—left no traces on Evreinov's work. Language
barriers may have been at issue here, but it could also be a
case in which the threshold of perception for such critiques
lay below the public eye. Readers who had no sympathy for

socialism—and Evreinov can confidently be counted among them—did not feel compelled to seek explanations and analyses of a nominally left-wing dictatorship in the left-wing press, of all places.

In Evreinov's case, this lack of interest is particularly striking. An example would be a quotation he draws from the first detailed and critical biography of Stalin, published in French in 1935 by the former French communist leader Boris Souvarine. How he quotes from the book is revealing: The phrasing found in *The Steps of Nemesis* is exactly the same as a quote translated from French in a book review by the Russian émigré journal *Novyi grad*.[30] Evreinov clearly preferred not to draw on this early analysis of Stalinism directly, as a systemic account, despite his diligent consultation of so many other sources. The correspondence suggests that Evreinov did not even read the book himself.

Similarly, Evreinov ignores the extensive analytical writings on Stalinism by the international Left Opposition in general and its work on the Moscow show trials in particular. For example, there are no clear references to Lev Sedov's *Red Book* on the Moscow Trial of 1936, which illuminated much of the background to the show trial and soundly refuted the phantasmagorical constructs of Stalin's prosecutors. Sedov's father and Stalin's primary adversary, Leon Trotsky, one of the first sound political analysts of Stalinism, is also represented by a single quotation, namely a bon mot uttered at a mass meeting in 1937 that suicide was a luxury in the dungeons of the secret police. This, in turn, morphs into the "living dead" figures of Zinoviev and Kamenev in the play, who,

---

30 Boris Souvarine, *Staline: Aperçu historique de bolshévisme [1935]* (Paris: Les Éditions Gérard Lebovici, 1985), 448; Georgii P. Fedotov, "BORIS SOUVARINE. Staline," *Novyi grad*, no. 10 (1935): 142–144.

as in hell, cannot escape their daily torment, denied the ability to commit suicide by Stalin's henchmen. Trotsky's speech was reprinted in his 1937 book *Stalin's Crimes*, but Evreinov may have taken it from the exile press, like the Souvarine quote mentioned above.[31]

Does this lack of a systematic analysis of Stalinism in Evreinov's arsenal mean that *The Steps of Nemesis* has nothing to tell us about Stalinism? Such a judgement would be an injustice to Evreinov and his view of the show trials. The final scene, the fictional dress rehearsal for the 3rd Moscow Trial, radically deconstructs not only the monstrous conspiracy fabrications of the show trials, but also the preceding parts of the play, many of which present a narrative that is as personality-driven as anything written by Bazhanov. When Yagoda, the main protagonist of not only the play but also of the first phase of the Great Terror and the show trials, states that he "no longer needs a mask," his admission quickly goes beyond demonstratively "taking off the mask" in the usual manner of sham confessions. At first he admits that he was only pretending to play the role of a Bolshevik, but only a few sentences later he drops the bombshell: everyone, everyone without exception, is only acting. "Some play the role of the 'noble fathers of the people,' some play the role of 'denunciators and traitors,' some play the role of 'femme fatale,' and some play the role of 'executioners'!" This covers the entire range of actions of the protagonists of *The Steps of Nemesis*. The conspiracy of the high-ranking Bolsheviks, in which the spectator participates voyeuristically over the course of the play, dissolves. The admirable serenity of the sister from Paris, the tragedy of Yagoda's lover—were all these just masks, too? And what is supposed to

---

31   Leo Trotzki, *Stalins Verbrechen* (Zurich: Jean Christophe-Verlag, 1937), 157.

be hidden behind them? Is there anything behind it at all? If you know Evreinov's theory of theater, the answer can only be: no. There are no "real" individuals with "truthful" motivations for action. Everything is staged, and everyone is playing a role.

With this open and radical conclusion, Evreinov comes closer to high Stalinism's ghostly world of masks than it might seem at first glance. Mask is superimposed on mask, depending on the situation and context, until the game of pretense is internalized to such an extent that it no longer conceals anything "real". One may call it, as the "Soviet Subjectivities" school has done, the "Stalinist self".[32] I find another idea perhaps more apt, however, which views the individual in Stalinism as a fluid subject situated in the given moment of action, constrained within various, but never absolute, constellations of trust and distrust.[33] Everyday dissembling was omnipresent and crucial to protect oneself and survive. Everyone played a role, a different one depending on the situation, and given the potentially lethal unpredictability of terror, they had no choice. Thus, Yagoda's revelation, and Evreinov's play as well, are not only an unmasking of the show trials, but ultimately also a parable of Stalinism as a social and cultural system.

32 Igal Halfin and Jochen Hellbeck, "Rethinking the Stalinist Subject: Stephen Kotkin's 'Magnetic Mountain' and the State of Soviet Historical Studies," *Jahrbücher für Geschichte Osteuropas* 44, no. 3 (1996): 456–463.
33 Compare Jonathan Waterlow, *It's Only a Joke, Comrade! Humour, Trust and Everyday Life Under Stalin* (Oxford: CreateSpace, 2018).